ELFRIDA
Elfrida Vipont Foulds
1902 to 1992

by
Susan V. Hartshorne

Quacks Books
Q

© Susan V. Hartshorne 2010

ISBN 978-1-904446-26-2

British Library Cataloguing in Publication Data
Susan V. Hartshorne 2010
Elfrida Vipont Foulds

Printed in 11 point Plantin Typeface
and published by
Quacks Books
Petergate
York YO1 7HU

Contents

Chapter		Page
	Introduction	1
1.	Early Days	3
2.	School	13
3.	Music	24
4.	Family Life	32
5.	World War II	42
6.	Post War Changes	49
7.	An Almost Full-time Author	58
8.	International Travels	68
	Epilogue	76
	Appendix - Published Works	78

List of Illustrations

	Page
Dorothy with Elfrida (nine weeks)	3
Mount Street Friends Meeting House	5
Edward with Elfrida (3 years)	6
Birch Lane, Longsight	6
Surrey Lodge	7
Ralph, Elfrida & Cedric, 1909	8
Tom with new car	9

	Page
Victoria Park gates	14
Dalton Hall	15
The Mount School	17
The Mount - Class III, 1916	19
Elfrida (1920s)	24
Elfrida and Percy on holiday	26
Augustus Milner	27
Climbing on Tryfan	29
Elfrida and Percy's Wedding	32
10 Anson Road, Victoria Park	33
Lecture Recitals	35
Elfrida with Robin and Carol at the seaside	38
Yealand Manor	42
Pupils at the school	44
Yealand Children's Orchestra	46
Green Garth	50
Four daughters	50
Elfrida with corgi, 1950s	51
The author at work	52
Family group	53
Yealand Friends Meeting House	55
Elfrida and corgi, 1960s	56
Edward and Dorothy	59
Swimming bath opening	66
Elfrida at Earlham College receiving her Honorary Degree	77

Introduction

MY FIRST memories of my Aunt Elfrida date from 1940 when I was taken to the Quaker evacuation school at Yealand Manor in North Lancashire where Elfrida was headmistress. To a four year old, away from home and abandoned by her parents - or so it felt - it was a relief to find a familiar welcoming face.

Story time at Yealand Manor School was memorable. Elfrida always held everyone spell-bound and made all the characters in her stories come alive. Later, during my time in York at The Mount School, I heard Elfrida speak on a number of occasions - both at the school and also when, as sixth formers, we visited Cumbria to learn about early Quakers. Later still, I heard her talk to adult audiences and I realised that it was not only school children who were spell-bound by what she had to say. In spite of her diminutive size and deceptively frail appearance, her surprisingly powerful voice was able to hold everyone's attention, and also to inspire them. She nearly always illustrated what she had to say by telling a story. Many of these stories are to be found in the books she wrote and I was delighted to receive them as regular Christmas presents.

I was born and grew up in Manchester - in the same house, attached to the same surgery that my father, his brother Ralph and their sister, Elfrida, had known. It remained my family home until my parents retired to Silverdale - a village only a very few miles from Yealand Conyers where Elfrida then lived. A few years after our marriage, my husband John was appointed Warden of Hulme Hall in Manchester but we soon had to move off site due to building work. The University gave us temporary refuge for two years in a house that they had recently acquired - by a happy coincidence it was 10 Anson Road: Percy and Elfrida's first married home!

1

I have received help and encouragement from many people when writing this biography. Elfrida herself helped me a great deal! She was a hoarder and kept almost everything - letters, notes, scripts of talks she gave, draft manuscripts, photographs, etc. I have found these extremely useful (particularly the slightly fictionalised unpublished account of her early childhood) and am glad that her daughters did not succumb to an urge to throw everything away. Her daughter Carol, her literary executor and the family archivist, kept some things and deposited the rest in the Deansgate branch of the Manchester University Rylands Library. So I spent many hours in that library and am grateful for the help I received from the staff there. The cover picture and the photograph of Elfrida receiving her honorary degree are reproduced with their permission. One former member of the library staff (Brenda Scragg) has written a couple of articles about Elfrida which I found extremely useful. I also spent a considerable amount of time talking to Elfrida's daughters - without their help I would not have known about or understood some aspects of Elfrida's life. And my manuscript has benefited greatly from Carol's editing skills.

In addition, I am grateful for the permission to use some of the images of old Manchester given to me by Manchester City Archives and Local Studies. I have enjoyed the co-operation of those who guard the archives of The Mount School, York and of Manchester High School for Girls. And I have been delighted to hear from all the people who have memories of Elfrida and who took the trouble to write and share these with me. I have not been able to include quotations from them all, but they have all helped me form the picture of Elfrida that I hope I have accurately presented here. Knowing that there were others who, like me, believed that Elfrida needed a biography has been an encouragement. By their useful suggestions and gentle enquiries as to how the work was progressing, Ted Milligan, Bill Sessions, David Blamires and others have been of inestimable assistance. Without the help of all these people, Elfrida's biography would not have been finished.

Susan V. Hartshorne

CHAPTER 1

Early Days

EDWARD VIPONT Brown wrote in his 'Reminiscences': 'I announced at the meeting of Overseers[1] at Mount Street that afternoon that a poor woman Friend who seemed short of clothes had come into the Meeting, and I wanted women overseers to look after her. They showed great interest and sympathy, until one Friend burst out laughing, and it dawned upon them all what had happened!' He was announcing the birth of his daughter, Elfrida Vipont, and the joke was typical. Later in life he was better known for the serious side of his character – for his lectures on different aspects of Quakerism and the numerous pamphlets he wrote, but at that time he was fond of sport and practical jokes; enjoyed cycling; foreign travel; and visits to the theatre with his beautiful young wife, Dorothy. Their son Cedric was born in 1896 and Ralph followed in 1898. Elfrida's arrival in July 1902 completed their family.

Both Elfrida's parents came from long established Quaker families. Her father was born in North Shields, although his widowed mother moved to York when

Dorothy with Elfrida (nine weeks)

---

1. Quakers who are responsible for pastoral care in their Meeting.

3

he was five years old so that he and his brothers could have an education at Bootham, a Quaker School. Edward enjoyed his time at Bootham and although he didn't shine at academic subjects, he made his mark on the sports field. He played in the first X1 football team and broke the school record for the mile. During one summer, when only 13 years old, he cycled with his two older brothers to Edinburgh and back on a 'penny farthing'. After leaving school, he qualified as a doctor in London where he helped establish a Quaker football team (the Foxes) and afterwards joined his cousin in general practice in Manchester.

Elfrida's mother (Dorothy Crowley) was born into a large family in Croydon; she was the thirteenth of fourteen children. She was also educated in York – at The Mount School. The Mount and Bootham have joint Old Scholars' activities and Dorothy met her future husband at their annual Whitsuntide gathering when she was still at school and aged only 14. It was love at first sight, but they had to wait five years before she had finished her education (which included some time in Switzerland) and had become old enough for him to ask for her hand in marriage. Some young men in her home town were not too happy that, as they said: 'the wolf from the north had carried off the belle of Croydon Quaker Meeting'. Not only was she beautiful, but she also had a strong character and advanced ideas about equality. Although not a militant suffragette, she was a strong supporter of the Women's Suffrage Movement and later a member of the Women's International League for Peace and Freedom.

Industrial Manchester with its smoke blackened buildings must have been at first quite a shock to Dorothy, and how did she view the discovery that her mother-in-law (Emily Brown) had chosen all her servants? Emily by that time had moved to Somerset, and had chosen a family from that part of the country to travel up north and look after the young couple. However, whatever her initial doubts, Dorothy soon realised that this was an excellent choice and Lizzie (the cook/housekeeper), Annie (the nursemaid) and Tom (the groom) became well-loved members of the family.

Edward and Dorothy were contemporaries of Rufus Jones and John Wilhelm Rowntree – Friends who helped to swing Quakerism away from the evangelical movement so that it became a much more liberal faith. Edward attended the significant 1895 Manchester Conference and they both took part in the Summer Schools in Scarborough and Birmingham that followed that Conference.

Mount Street Friends Meeting House[2] is in the centre of Manchester and Elfrida's parents thought it was very old-fashioned when they first joined. The building itself seemed grim, guarded by tall iron railings with forbidding spikes. Inside, the sexes were rigidly separated. After passing through a large communal lobby, men and women proceeded by separate entrances – men on the right, women on the left – into the large meeting room. This was a vast hall with upper galleries to the right and left and with seating facing the meeting for the elders and ministers. Heat came up through iron gratings in the centre gangway. Edward and Dorothy were determined to make some changes and decided, as a first step, to defy convention and sit together. Dorothy firmly sat down next to Edward. Soon others followed their example. At that time children of all ages had to sit through the full hour of Meeting for Worship. Later, when she had children of her own, Dorothy introduced another change

Mount Street Friends Meeting House, 1900

---

2. Now known as Central Manchester Quaker Meeting House.

– children's classes on alternate Sundays. However, Elfrida later wrote that she didn't mind the long silences in Meeting. She often used the time to make up stories – sometimes about the people she saw around her. Her first memories of that Meeting were that all the elderly women Friends wore bonnets and many of the men wore beards!

The Brown's house, Surrey Lodge, was in Birch Lane, Longsight, on the outskirts of Manchester and there was at that time open country at the end of the road. The house was opposite an old public house – the Wagon and Horses – and near the junction of Stockport Road and Plymouth Grove. The wide streets, paved with stone setts, were lit by gas lamps; tram lines ran down the centre of the main roads; and wires stretched overhead to which the tram trolleys were

Edward with Elfrida (3 years)

Birch Lane, Longsight

attached. The doctors' surgery was at one side of the house through a connecting door, and it included a dispensary where medicines were prepared.

From the dispensary, a window opened into the waiting room through which patients would collect their medicines – in bottles which were carefully corked, covered with white paper and sealed with red sealing wax, or in pill boxes of many different sizes. As a special treat, Elfrida was sometimes allowed to sit on the high stool in the dispensary to play with the corks and pill boxes.

Surrey Lodge

A very large picture of Elizabeth Fry in Newgate prison surrounded by women prisoners and their children hung in the consulting room next door – perhaps to remind the patients that there were many others much worse off than themselves. Similarly large pictures adorned the walls of the main house – William Penn and the Indians were on the upstairs landing; Elizabeth Fry guarded the bottom of the stairs; pictures of John Bright and John Dalton decorated the nursery walls.

Elfrida was not allowed to play out in the street on her own, but from an early age, she loved to watch the interesting things that went on there from the safety of her home. She envied the children swinging on the lamp posts even though they were poorly dressed and often had no shoes. She watched the trams that sometimes lost their trolleys and the trolley boys who jumped out to put them back on the wires; the organ grinder with his monkey; the rag and bone man; and in the evening, the lamplighter lighting the gas lamps. Occasionally the horse-drawn fire engine rushed past with the smartly clad fireman clanging the bell; and sometimes people came to take a ride in the 'growlers' – the cabs that lined up outside the Wagon and Horses.

Ralph, Elfrida and Cedric, 1909

When she grew a little older she was allowed to go with her brothers to spend some of her pocket money on sweets from the shop round the corner. One penny would buy 4 ozs of aniseed balls, fruit drops, acid drops or humbugs. The choice was so difficult.

Horses (Prince George and Princess Mary) were stabled in the back yard. Elfrida loved to give them apples. Their groom, Tom Salter, looked after them and sometimes she persuaded him to lift her up and let her ride across the yard. Tom took her father out in the trap every day on his 'rounds' – as the daily visits to patients were called – and being allowed to go with them was one of Elfrida's favourite outings. While her father visited his patients, Tom would look after her and tell her stories. Both her father and Tom wore top hats and she thought them very smart. Her father also wore a frock coat, a shirt with starched collar and cuffs, and a waistcoat with a gold watch and chain. Later, when he got an assistant who wore a lounge suit and soft hat, Elfrida could not, at first, believe that he was a proper doctor.

One day there was great excitement. Outside the house was a green Armstrong-Siddeley motorcar with red upholstery. Elfrida was excited too, but then she was told that Prince George and Princess Mary would have to be sold so that the car could be garaged in their stables. For a while she was inconsolable, but then came to enjoy her rides in the smart new car. Her father never learnt to drive, but it didn't take long for Tom to acquire this new skill and to turn into a chauffeur. There were no driving

Tom with new car

tests then but a change of clothing was needed and he wore a peaked cap and green overcoat.

Every morning a gong in the hall would be sounded at 7.45 am – making the family aware that a full cooked breakfast awaited them. Afterwards all (including the servants) shared a short period of silent prayer and a bible reading. Their main meal was taken in the middle of the day and afternoon tea at 5.0 pm consisted of bread and butter, home-made jam, cakes and scones. Each meal started with a silent grace. Elfrida's parents, like many older Quakers at that time, used 'plain' speech. That is, they used 'thee' and 'thou' for the second person singular instead of the more usual 'you'. The reason for this was that in earlier centuries, because they believed in treating all people alike, Quakers had refused to call the rich and powerful people 'you' (as they thought their rank demanded) and the poor 'thou'. By the 20th century this practice had ceased to be so meaningful and increasingly Quakers ceased to use plain language. However, Elfrida used it throughout her life – though mainly to family members and fellow Quakers.

Most of the time Elfrida and her brothers played in the 'day nursery'. This was a large room on the first floor where there was a much loved rocking horse, a doll's house and lots of books. However, she also enjoyed being with Lizzie in the kitchen – watching milk being ladled out of a big can by the milkman into Lizzie's bowl, or seeing her making butter balls with the butter pats.

Every week day, unless it was pouring with rain, the children were all taken out for a walk. At the end of Birch Lane there were fields and a farm with a duck pond to be explored. Often they went to Birch Park or Platt Fields, a much larger park. Both were within walking distance of Surrey Lodge. Sometimes they went instead to visit cousins or friends who lived near by.

During the week Dorothy would sometimes hold an 'At Home' and Elfrida wore a special dress and helped by handing round the cakes. The Misses Gaskell (Elizabeth Gaskell's daughters), were among those who came to those occasions. The Gaskells lived very near Surrey Lodge.

Sundays were different. Edward went off early to Adult School – helping to lead discussions for a class of working men who had missed out on education. This ended only just in time for him to go straight to Mount Street Quaker Meeting in the centre of the city. So, usually it was their mother who took Elfrida and her brothers to Meeting. They went on the top deck of an electric tram-car and their father came later. In the afternoon, Dorothy also took an Adult School class. Elfrida grew up with an intense dislike of the Adult School Movement because it was responsible for taking away her parents for such a large part of each weekend. The children were not allowed to play with their toys on Sundays though books were allowed. On Sunday afternoons their parents often held open house for students from Dalton Hall - the Quaker University Hall of Residence in Manchester.

Elfrida's brothers, Cedric and Ralph, usually played together and often didn't have a great deal of time for their little sister. Mr. Batters, Elfrida's imaginary friend, always had plenty of time. He lived by the side of the nursery fire and always gave the sort of advice that she wanted to hear. He was pleased to listen to Elfrida's made-up stories even if others didn't have the time. She wrote later: 'Nothing would stop me from telling stories. My long-suffering family and friends must have sighed with relief when at last I became capable of writing them down, so that my captive audience could be left in peace.'

Elfrida slept in her parent's room until she was about six or seven years old and said her prayers every night before going to sleep. She loved to hear her parents talking when they had come upstairs to get ready for going out in the evening and she pretended she was asleep so they wouldn't notice that she was listening. Her mother always looked so beautiful when she was dressed ready to go out. If Elfrida woke early in the morning her father would tell her stories - stories about his childhood in North Shields, though she couldn't imagine that he had ever been a child. He told her about the excitement he had felt when seeing the first iron ship sail down the River Tyne and about his cousins' black nurse who had escaped from being held as a slave in America and who helped look after him. She loved listening to stories.

Every summer Dorothy and the children went by train to Croydon to stay with Granny Crowley at Bramley Oaks. This was, in comparison to Surrey Lodge, a very large and splendid house with extensive grounds - including tennis courts, many lawns and a kitchen garden. There was even a little house for the gardener. There were always cousins to play with and lots of aunts and uncles who had time to spare for their little niece. Aunt Emma in particular, created another world for Elfrida through the stories she told her. Everyone enjoyed the picnics in the hayfields. At Bramley Oaks she got to know some other interesting members of her family – Aunt Maud, for example, was one of London University's early women graduates and visited schools investigating cases of truancy and distributing relief to poor families with school age children, Aunt Mabel was one of the first women members of Meeting for Sufferings (the Quaker national executive body) and Aunt Muriel was one of the first women magistrates. Regular visits were also paid to relatives in Alton (Hampshire) and to Granny Brown who kept house for her son Uncle William, a vet, in Somerset.

Unlike many Quakers at that time who disapproved of theatres, Elfrida's parents enjoyed outings to concerts and to the theatre and often invited their musical friends to their home. So their children also were encouraged when they were old enough to take advantage of the many entertainments that Manchester had to offer, including Hallé concerts and Gilbert and Sullivan operas. Elfrida particularly enjoyed the Lord Mayor's Christmas party - white party dresses were worn and there was a magic lantern, a conjuror and dancing to a piano. This was a great treat as no piano was allowed at the Quaker Meeting House and there they had to make do with a bell when they played musical chairs and other games.

Elfrida loved going shopping with her mother and also with her father, who took her to the bookshop and bought her books. After she had made her choice, Elfrida watched the metal container with the bill and money in it whizzing round the ceiling on a wire until it reached the young lady in a glass box[3]. After shopping they would go to Meng & Eckers for tea with cream buns.

At Surrey Lodge the weekly washing was done in the cellar in several large tubs, and the children sometimes played down there. From the main cellar a small door opened into what Elfrida's brothers called the caverns. It was just an unlit storage space but the boys told frightening ghost stories about the black bogey who lived there. Elfrida was scared stiff and this, no doubt, played at least some part in her recurring 'fantasmas' as she called them. These were nightmares and sometimes also irrational daytime fears - her vivid imagination led her to think, for example, that the lions would escape from the zoo or that she would fall through the ice when skating on the lake. However, her imaginary friend, Mr. Batters, helped to reassure her and he was particularly valued when her brothers went away to school.

At the age of nine, Cedric went away to Stramongate, a Quaker preparatory school in Kendal. This felt like the breaking up of Elfrida's world. He had, of course, been attending a local school for some time, but to be away for months at a time was something different. Shortly afterwards Ralph became very ill with typhoid and Elfrida was sent to stay with her Cousin Nell who lived close by in Dickenson Road. Fortunately Ralph recovered after a time of convalescence but when later he, too, went away to Stramongate he became ill again. Elfrida was told that he had twice nearly died and her vivid imagination created fears and 'fantasmas' that would take some time to resolve. However, by that time she had started school and a different life was beginning to open up for her.

---

3. A usual method of payment in large shops in the first half of the 20th century. The young lady would send the change (if any) back the same way.

CHAPTER 2

School

WHEN SHE was five, Elfrida followed her brothers to Aucklands School. Aucklands was in Victoria Park, on the corner of Denison Road and Lower Park Road, and was within walking distance of Surrey Lodge. It was a preparatory school for Manchester High School for Girls and South Manchester Grammar School for Boys – boys and girls were taught together. The brochure describes the work of the school as being 'especially directed towards the formation of character, the development of intelligence and interest and the provision of a thorough education preparatory to Upper School work.' In carrying out these aims it stressed that 'special care is taken to avoid over-stimulation and pressure.' So in addition to more academic subjects, every day there was drill out of doors – weather permitting. The prospectus was endorsed by Miss Gaskell and by John William Graham (Principal of Dalton Hall). Elfrida was glad that Ralph had still a year left at Aucklands when she started. She felt safer knowing that he could easily be reached if needed.

On her way backwards and forwards to school she passed through the Victoria Park gates – exchanging greetings with the toll keepers, who collected money from vehicles that went through the park. The money from the tolls was used to keep the roads in good repair as Victoria Park (and the repair of its roads) was not adopted by the City Council until the 1950s.

Elfrida continued to enjoy listening to the stories that both her parents read to her. She loved books by Beatrix Potter, Mrs. Ewing and E Nesbit and eagerly waited for their new books to be published. Once when the family were on holiday in the Lake District, they passed through Far Sawrey (where Beatrix Potter

Victoria Park gates (Daisy Bank Road/Plymouth Grove junction)

lived) and Elfrida was sure she saw Peter Rabbit squeezing under the gate. Her mother also read Kipling's *Jungle Book* and the *Just So Stories* to her although her father didn't like Kipling because of his militarism. Later *Little Women* and other books by Louisa M Alcott became her favourites. She soon learnt to read these for herself and read them over and over again.

She shared her passion for these books with Rachel Graham and her brothers and sisters. The Graham family lived at Dalton Hall where their father was Principal. The Hall was in Victoria Park quite near Elfrida's new school and housed students who were mainly studying at Manchester University. Like the Browns, the Grahams were Quakers and members of Mount Street Meeting. Rachel was about eighteen months older than Elfrida and became her special friend. Their 'Hawthorn Club' was inspired by *Little Women* and they all wrote stories and plays and produced a magazine from time to time. They enacted scenes from *Little Women* and Rachel Graham remembers 'Elfrida in her brother's clothes as Laurie'. Elfrida wrote several plays (*'The Trio'*, *'Young Macdonell'*, and *'The Ransome'*). Another called *'The Wicked Baron'* they performed for the children at the University Settlement in Ancoats. They loved playing all sorts of make-believe games – in the garden if fine, and in the fives court at Dalton Hall if wet. They played Roundheads and

14

Dalton Hall, 1910

Cavaliers, Bonnie Prince Charlie, Robin Hood and any game involving knights and castles. They also gave musical concerts to their families. Rachel was at Aucklands with Elfrida and like her she went on to Manchester High School; and then to The Mount School in York.

Elfrida's talent for writing was encouraged by Aucklands School and she received 23 out of a possible 25 marks for 'Writing' in one end of term report. She was also, at that time, learning to play the piano. Her teacher was Miss Emily Follows, and in 1912 she successfully took her first piano exam – the first of many. Although she enjoyed her piano lessons, she couldn't understand why Cedric, who refused to continue with his lessons, was able happily to strum tunes by ear that he had only heard once or twice, while she found it necessary to learn every note. And his 'strumming', although it annoyed his parents, provided great entertainment for his friends. Later Cedric had lessons on the cello and played this in a more conventional way – throughout his life he was to enjoy playing in various amateur orchestras.

In 1912, after five years at Aucklands, Elfrida moved to the Junior department of Manchester High School for Girls. This was a very different experience. High School girls wore uniform – a gym tunic which had to be one inch from the ground when you were kneeling down and a white blouse or jersey. There was also a broad-brimmed boater with yellow hatband, edged with black lines, and adorned with a shield in front bearing the letters MHSG. Elfrida was immensely proud of her school hat. Discipline was much stricter – no running in the corridors was allowed, uniforms and hair had to be kept tidy – and there were so many girls that she found it, at first, quite bewildering. Rachel was already at the school but, of course, being older was in a different class although they met in the playground at lunchtime. However, Elfrida soon got used to the daily routine. She may have found it restricting to her imagination at the time, but later she came to value the sound grounding she received at the High School in all aspects of grammar.

She particularly enjoyed the singing lessons, learning to sing in parts, and she grew very fond of Miss Precious who both taught her singing and was also Head of the Junior School.

In history lessons great stress was laid on the importance of the British Empire and Elfrida soon became familiar with the large map of the world which showed bright red British patches in many different places.

Elfrida was still at the High School during the first year of World War 1. Before it began, she had helped her parents send out circulars urging peace by negotiation and had listened to their discussions about the Quaker peace testimony. She was proud to be allowed to address one of the circulars to the King and Queen at Buckingham Palace. As soon as war was declared, her older brother Cedric, who had just finished his Matriculation Examination, volunteered to serve in the Friends Ambulance Unit. After training at Jordans in Buckinghamshire, he crossed to France in January 1915 and his letters home were eagerly awaited. Elfrida could see that although her parents were proud of him, they were also very worried.

She wrote later that she would always be

....proud to remember that I was present at the huge Peace meeting held in the Free Trade Hall. It should have been held in Mount Street Meeting House but a few nervous Friends objected because one of the speakers was to be Ramsay Macdonald and they feared he would attract violence....

The hall was well filled …. He spoke about the unity of all mankind in God…..I remembered ever since the atmosphere of worship'.

Elfrida soon learnt that most of the girls at the High School did not have families who thought and acted like hers. They all seemed to support the war and when troops marched down Dover Street, the whole class would stand up and salute, even though they could not be seen. They were told to learn Rudyard Kipling's poem *'Oh, where are you going to, all you big steamers?'* but her father refused to let her learn it and wrote to the Headmistress saying it was bad poetry and bad morals. She had to remain sitting at her desk while all her classmates stood up and recited it at her! She hoped she was suffering for the Peace Testimony!

After two years in the junior department of the High School, a decision had to be made as to where Elfrida was to continue her education. Should she move into the senior school or go to The Mount School and join her brother, Ralph, in York? As a result of her final examinations in the Junior School, she was awarded the Hulme Foundation Scholarship which would help pay for three years in the senior school and there was therefore good reason to stay in Manchester. However, after some discussion

The Mount School

her parents decided not to take this scholarship up but to follow family tradition and send her to The Mount. Probably the peace issues had something to do with the decision.

Although York was quite some distance from Manchester, The Mount School was already familiar to Elfrida. Both her mother and her grandmother had been pupils at the school – not to mention numerous aunts and cousins. The family regularly attended Old Scholars' gatherings and she had also visited her brothers at Bootham School. In addition, she had a number of relatives who lived in York.

The Mount had already adjusted to a wartime routine. Clifford Street Friends Meeting House[4] had been requisitioned for use as a hospital so for Sunday morning Meeting for Worship about half York Friends joined Bootham pupils at that school and half went to The Mount. Most of the girls (and the staff) had brothers, fathers or other relatives who were involved in the war in some way and everyone dreaded the notification of bad news. Elfrida described her first experience of a Zeppelin raid at the beginning of her second term (in 1916):

> I was having what seemed to be a very disturbing kind of dream and awoke to find Miss Collyer begging me to wake up. The bombs were dropping, making a deafening noise, and there were flashes of light which lit up the room. We all jumped out of bed and ran downstairs barefooted, to collect in a shivering group in Miss Graham's sitting-room. That was the worst of all the raids, and a great deal of damage was done, some of it quite near the school.

Ralph left school in the summer of 1916 and joined the Friends War Victims Relief Service. He was too young to be sent abroad at first, so after training he worked in the UK – mainly in London. Soon after his 18th birthday he was sent to work in France.

Food rationing (at first just of bread, meat and sugar) was introduced in 1916 and although there was never any danger of starvation, at times the school had difficulty in providing more than very basic meals. Elfrida didn't have a very big appetite, and

---

4. Now known as Friargate Quaker Meeting House.

The Mount – Class III, 1916
(Elfrida is second from the left on the back row)

she remembered that she was often able to let others have some of her ration.

But she later wrote:

> I often wonder whether people fully realise how it affected the children in their teens who were at school. It wasn't only the effect of rationing, and Zeppelin raids and so on, it was the effect of big issues bearing down upon us, when we were old enough to realise and appreciate them, but not old enough to grasp them.

Elfrida maintained a lifelong admiration for Winifred Sturge, the Headmistress, who, in spite of the war, managed to ensure that ordinary school life went on much as usual. Every morning there was a text to be learned before breakfast – a few biblical verses or perhaps some classical poetry. Like many other Mount girls, Elfrida didn't enjoy learning texts at the time, but the practice provided her memory with a store of quotations for which she was to be eternally grateful.

Elfrida developed her talent for drawing and took, and passed with honours, the examinations of the Royal Drawing Society. Soon after she arrived in York she joined the school archaeological society and went on various school trips, discovering and getting to know all the Yorkshire treasures such as the abbeys at Whitby, Rievaulx and Fountains. She kept a notebook in which she drew sketches of the architectural features that she most admired.

Elfrida's health was not good and in 1914 she spent some time convalescing with relatives in Grange-over-Sands. There didn't seem to be anything very seriously wrong with her, although she often had nose bleeds and once had a suspected thrombosis while she was at The Mount. However, her health problems were enough to excuse her from games. She didn't mind this a bit! So when everyone else was busy exercising, she was allowed to follow her archaeological hobby and wander round York visiting old churches and filling her notebook with sketches. As long as she told the school where she was going and brought back her notebook filled with appropriate sketches, she was allowed a considerable amount of freedom.

When she was at home on holiday, she continued to follow her interest in architecture. She cycled to Prestbury to see the Norman chapel there; when the family holidayed in North Wales, her notebook was filled with a detailed description of Conway Castle and the Cromlech on The Great Orme; and when she stayed in Grange she visited Cartmel Priory.

She studied piano with Herbert Golden. The Mount was lucky to have him on the staff – and so was Elfrida. He was teaching at Frankfurt Conservatorium before the war, but was in England when war broke out and was unable to return to Germany. Elfrida wrote home about her feelings before her first lesson – 'I'm a jelly, a saturated sponge, a worm on the ground' but then afterwards 'it's over, and he's absolutely topping'. Elfrida also enjoyed her singing lessons and sang alto both in the school choir, and in the joint choir with Bootham. Later her voice was described as soprano or mezzo soprano, but probably she sang alto because the school had difficulty in finding enough people who were able to read music and follow the alto line.

Early in her time at The Mount she played and sang in one of the many school concerts. She wrote home: 'I sat quietly at the piano for a few seconds and then I played a few bars of *'All through the Night'* very softly. I sang it through and then went to my place and then – oh mother – they clapped and stamped and thumped and Miss Grubb told me to sing the last verse again.'

Shortly after this concert Elfrida succumbed to some virus and, while she was in the Nursery *(the sick bay)*, a member of staff asked what her hobbies were. She answered 'writing' and the suggestion was made that she should write for the school magazine. This was the beginning of numerous articles, plays and reports written for the magazine. She wrote about her brother (and other girls' brothers) in the Friends Ambulance Unit (FAU) and said 'Imagination can picture the many terrible and exciting things they have experienced caused by bombs and shells'. She also wrote about her home and holidays, about the 1916 Irish Rising and the occupation of Jacob's biscuit factory; a story about a stolen dog; one about Samuel the black cat; a play about VADs[5] – and she also wrote a long ballad entitled 'Christabel'. She enjoyed performing in the school plays as well as writing them and took the part of the Prince in Mark Twain's 'The Prince and the Pauper'.

She was glad she had relatives in York and could therefore spend some time away from the school relaxing with her cousins, the Adams family, at The White House in Fulford. She hurried there when at last Armistice was declared, only to find that they – along with many other York residents – had gone to the Minster to give thanks. The school celebrated the end of the war a few days later by everyone dressing up and staging a model League of Nations with delegates from every country.

In 1918, soon after Elfrida arrived home that Christmas, Cedric also returned – his service in the FAU having now come to an end. It was marvellous to see him but he was suffering from the effects of gas, and it was clear he would need to spend some time convalescing before he was completely fit again. Two days later they all went to the station to meet Ralph who was home on leave. Although they knew he was going to return to France in the New Year, the whole family celebrated the end of the war and looked forward to a peaceful future together. They

---

5. 'Voluntary Aid Detachments' provided medical assistance in time of war. Two thirds of the VADs in WW1 were women and girls working as, for example, assistant nurses and ambulance drivers.

enjoyed visits to the opera, to concerts and to parties as well as attending more serious meetings where Cedric spoke about the FAU and Ralph spoke about the work he had been doing with the Friends War Victims Relief service and what still needed to be done. They all went into town to see President Wilson when he came to visit Manchester. Ralph wrote in his diary that that Christmas Day was 'the happiest we have had for many a year'. He crossed back to France on 21 January. It was to be the last time they would all be together.

In March 1919 they received the devastating news of Ralph's death. He had succumbed to the influenza that eventually succeeded in killing more people than had been slaughtered in the war. His parents received a letter telling them he was ill and his father hurried to Calais, leaving Dorothy, who was herself seriously ill with the 'flu. Tragically, by the time he got there, Ralph had died and had been buried in Les Baraques Military Cemetery in Sangatte. It seemed particularly cruel that he should have survived the dangers of the war, only to succumb to the 'flu.

Elfrida was at school when she heard the news and her feelings are reflected in the poem she wrote and which she sent to her parents, the last verse of which is:

> I hail thy spirit in the wind
> That tears these empty mists apart,
> Thy laugh rings through eternity
> To stab the sorrow in my heart.

The shock of Ralph's death prolonged Dorothy's illness and it was not until the autumn that she was fit enough to travel to France to see his grave.

It says much for Elfrida's strength of character that she continued her studies and passed her Matriculation Examination in 1919. There were then prolonged discussions about her future. She wanted to spend some time in Paris but her mother said this was 'quite out of the present calculation'. So Elfrida threw herself into the many and varied activities which took place during her last year at school as well as studying hard for her Higher School Certificate – she achieved this in July 1920 (French, English and History). She undertook major roles in two school plays, sang in concerts and wrote a number of articles and reviews for the school magazine. She also played a full part in the Leavers' celebrations which marked the end of her school years.

In 1920, very soon after leaving school, Elfrida went with Cedric to the International Young Friends' Conference at Jordans and this made a lasting impression on her. They both found it an occasion which they would long remember. They were particularly glad to be able to welcome a contingent of German Young Friends to the gathering and they were inspired by hearing Rufus Jones speak.

The conference had made Elfrida think seriously about the Quaker beliefs and traditions that she had inherited. She knew she had to make her own decisions but was not yet sure that Quakerism was the right way for her.

CHAPTER 3

Music

BY THE autumn of 1919 Dorothy's health had improved sufficiently for Edward to take her to see Ralph's grave and the places where he had been working – to Sermaize and to the maternity hospital at Chalons-sur-Marne. Afterwards, escaping from Manchester's winter weather, they spent a relaxing holiday in the South of France. When they returned home, discussions continued about Elfrida's future and now a short time in Paris did not seem so out of the question. It was finally arranged that she should spend three months in Paris before starting at Manchester University to read history. In Paris she was to follow her two main interests – music and history – and also improve her French.

Paris opened up a new world for Elfrida. She stayed with a friend at 27 Avenue du Marechal Foch in St Cloud, attended history lectures and singing lessons and her French improved dramatically. She studied singing with Madame Laute-Brun and sang two songs in a concert arranged by Madame as a showcase for her pupils. She visited the Hotel Britannique where both her brothers had stayed on their way to and from France during the war and was welcomed by the

Elfrida, 1920s

Baxters who were the proprietors. In her free time she wandered round churches and galleries and in the evenings often went to the theatre. She also did a lot of thinking about her future. She wrote home about a visit she made to a church in St Etienne du Mont where she had an experience that she was later to describe as something very special, 'I experienced something very real there, what, I can hardly tell thee, save that I know now what I am going to do and I understand about the different kinds of worship, and the relationship in which I stand to them.' Looking back she understood this to be a turning point in her life.

She came home at the end of September to prepare for the start of the University term in October and to join in the activities of the thriving group of Manchester Young Friends. Many of them had seen active Quaker service during the war and were eager to help build a more peaceful future. They produced a monthly periodical, *Searchlight*, to which Elfrida contributed.

Elfrida enjoyed her first year at university and was to have a lifelong interest in history. However, she gradually began to realise that unless she soon continued her studies in music, she would probably lose the progress she had made in Paris and, perhaps, never realise her ambition to embark on a career as a singer. She discussed this with Cedric and with her parents. Cedric was sympathetic but their parents took a lot of convincing even though she told them that Madame Laute-Brun had encouraged her to pursue this career.

In 1921, it was Cedric's second year as a medical student at Manchester. He brought home to Surrey Lodge many of the Dalton Hall students, and often took Elfrida along to the numerous social events in the Hall. Cedric had served in the FAU with Teddy Foulds and so both he and Elfrida soon got to know Teddy's older brother, Percy, who was resident at Dalton Hall while reading Chemistry at the University. Elfrida enjoyed Percy's company but although later their friendship was to deepen, at that time she didn't see him as anything more than a friend – among many others.

The Foulds family were mill owners in Colne (Lancashire) and although not Quakers they sent Percy and his brothers to Ackworth – a Quaker School in South Yorkshire. During the war

Percy served in the FAU, first at the Star and Garter Hospital for paraplegics in Richmond and then in the hospital at Dunkirk.

For some time Elfrida's parents had wanted to visit the Austrian Tyrol but of course had been unable to do so because of the war. They planned to spend three weeks there in the summer of 1922 and to take Cedric and Elfrida with them. They all spent many happy hours in planning where they would go and who they would meet. But, only a short time before they were due to go, Edward's partner fell ill and he therefore didn't feel he could leave the practice. Rather than cancel the whole trip, at short notice two others were found to take their place – Percy Foulds and Oliver Holdsworth. So instead of the rather sedate tour as planned, it turned into something quite different! They left their worries and some of their inhibitions at home and they thoroughly enjoyed themselves. Elfrida found Percy a delightful companion and their friendship developed. She wrote an account of their trip (unpublished) entitled *'Four Innocents Abroad'*. In addition to countless stops to allow Cedric to take photographs

Elfrida and Percy on holiday

or Elfrida to examine some architectural feature, they had plenty of time to 'stop and stare', to have fun and to play numerous games of cards. On the way back they visited Ralph's grave near Calais.

Eventually Elfrida's persuasion won over her parents and they agreed that if she left the University they would help her fulfil her dreams of a musical career. They spent some considerable time and correspondence finding out how best to make this dream come true. It was decided eventually that she should study in London with Augustus Milner and his wife Dora. He taught singing and his wife, piano. Augustus Milner had studied singing in Berlin and Prague, was brought to London by Thomas Beecham in 1919, and had worked in opera with both Covent Garden and the British National Opera Company. Elfrida's mother took her for an interview and audition with them and she sang

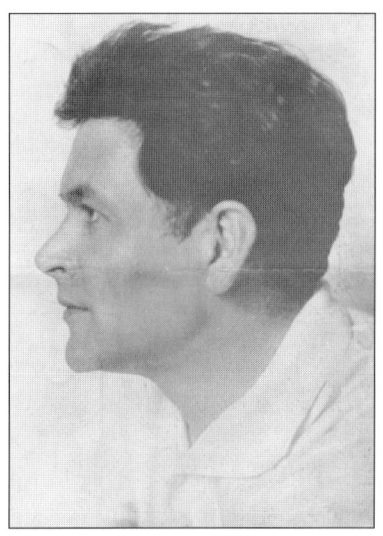

Augustus Milner

'*Voi che sapete*' (from *Mozart's Figaro*). Dorothy wrote home to Edward and said 'I asked whether he *(Augustus Milner)* thought we were justified in letting her take up singing professionally and he had no doubt whatever about it. He says three years training is the least – she must be prepared for that.' She certainly was prepared for that. Augustus Milner said 'I shall be glad to begin work with your daughter on April 16th'. So that's when she started – after spending some time visiting a school friend in Denmark whose father was Principal of one of the Danish Folk High Schools.

In London, Elfrida at first stayed at the Minerva Club in Brunswick Square. Then when her cousin Beryl Crowley came to London they shared a flat in 49 Princes Gate. London was an exciting place to be in the 1920s. After the wartime years there was much rejoicing and a relaxing of the previous enforced austerity. Elfrida's circle of friends widened; although she worked hard at her musical studies, there were lots of young people of her age to share her time with; and her life was full of interest. The Milners led a bohemian existence – in many ways different from the life Elfrida had been used to. They took Elfrida into their family and they even managed to teach her to cook – a little! She had never had to cook for herself and was not really very interested in food. However, she did learn how to make coffee, omelettes and spaghetti with tomato sauce.

Although their relationship had not at that time developed very far, Percy wrote to Elfrida on at least a couple of occasions while she was in London, letting her know (among other things) that he had been made a tutor at Dalton Hall.

By 1923, Elfrida's musical education was advancing very satisfactorily. The Milners worked her hard and she practised every day. They also took her to concerts and at the end of the evening she often went back to their house to talk through what she had seen and heard, and sometimes stayed the night with them.

In February she sang in the Wigmore Hall in a concert given by all Augustus Milner's pupils. The exhilarating experience gave her a taste of what might be in store if her singing career progressed. Her parents noted that 'Many people have told us they were delighted with Elfrida's singing at the Wigmore Hall.'

In June her parents at last got their delayed holiday. They went to France and on the way stopped to see Elfrida's flat in Princes Gate and also called on the Milners. After visiting Ralph's grave they holidayed in various places, including Aix and Avignon. When they were on their way home Elfrida travelled to Paris to meet them. Her father had to return home to work, but her mother stayed and enjoyed a few days being shown around Paris by her daughter.

Later in the summer Cedric and Elfrida spent some time on Skye together. They were both now members of the Fell and Rock Climbing Club and they enjoyed both the challenges presented by the mountains and the magnificent views from their summits. They wrote home enthusiastically: 'The peak we went up today was fine. We did a long ridge walk the first day and then on the second day, a round of smaller and 'safe' mountains as bad weather'. Cedric took lots of photographs – photography was one of his major hobbies. In the next few years, they had a number of other short climbing holidays together – conquering many of the Lake District and North Wales peaks.

Climbing on Tryfan, North Wales, 1921

In September 1924 the Milners thought Elfrida was ready for her first public appearance. This was not just a student concert; she was performing as a professional. She sang in Welwyn Garden City accompanied by Dora Milner and shared the concert with Anthony Maney, another of the Milners' students. The criticism was mixed but quite encouraging. 'Miss Vipont opens her mouth beautifully. She should learn to act a little more powerfully'. Then she enthusiastically accepted a number of invitations to sing at schools and meeting houses – she sang at Leighton Park School, at Alton and at Scarborough. However, the Milners were not pleased that she was taking on this sort of commitment and said, 'It doesn't do to mix with amateurs!' They thought it might damage her professional career.

In November she was a minor soloist in a performance of Elijah with the South London Philharmonic Society – she sang the part of the boy and received three guineas. Augustus Milner took the main solo part. In January 1925 she sang in the Barn Theatre, Oxted, as part of the Milner Vocal Quartet – with Jean Roper, John Patterson and Augustus Milner.

At that time there was among Quakers much discussion about whether the Arts had anything to contribute to worship and the spiritual life. Elfrida wrote to *The Friend* on 23.5.25:

In art as in life we must fix our gaze upon the highest which is revealed to us. We may be called to give our testimony in theatre, opera-house or concert hall, but in so far as we remain faithful to the Light our service is one with all service for the Kingdom, for the inmost pulses of art throb in the heart of worship. To some of us in the Society of Friends it is given to follow the way in Art, to the best of our ability.

For many of the older Friends, that was a revolutionary gospel.

Not surprisingly Elfrida's proud parents tried to get to all her concerts and were happy with the progress she was making. They wanted her to perform in Manchester so that their friends could more easily get to hear her, and so in March she sang in the Houldsworth Hall. She was clearly not in the best of health at the time and was suffering from nose bleeds. Perhaps not surprisingly the performance was not one of her best and she didn't receive a very good write-up. However, the visit to Manchester gave her an opportunity to go home and see her family and friends including Percy.

In April, Elfrida and Percy announced their engagement. In early May Percy visited her in London and, not surprisingly, she notes that they had a fantastic time together – 'it all grows more wonderful every day and seems even more right'. A few days later she wrote: 'I know that Percy and I are always together. I felt it during Meeting at Westminster yesterday'.

They planned to marry in a year's time but first Elfrida had an important concert to prepare for. On 28 October she was again to sing in the Wigmore Hall. However, this time she was no longer singing as one of Augustus Milner's students but as a professional in her own right and as such she needed an agent who would be responsible for all her future business arrangements. She chose as her London agent Lionel Powell & Holt and for her Manchester concerts she used Forsyths – the music store and publishers on Deansgate. Her programme for the Wigmore Hall included arias and songs by Caldara, Haydn, Mozart, Schumann, Franz and Quilter and she was accompanied by John Wills. The next day's papers carried favourable notices. *The Times* said she 'showed promise' though 'her technique is more advanced than her powers of interpretation'. The *Telegraph's* reviewer said she had 'afforded a considerable measure of enjoyment' and that it was 'all too rare an experience to encounter a singer possessed of so unfailing a sense of tunefulness – well ordered technique, consistent charm if of no particular variety'. The *Westminster Gazette* noted that she had a 'bright, fresh voice, engaging simplicity, excellent training and with further experience should carry her far'. Everyone was pleased with this encouraging response.

Unfortunately a concert with a fairly similar programme given in the Houldsworth Hall in Manchester on 15 February 1926 was not so well received. The *Manchester Guardian* thought Elfrida 'possibly has a better love for speech than for music' although they noted that 'We have not heard the last of Miss Vipont by a long way.' Although she and her family were a little downcast, Augustus Milner was satisfied that she was progressing well. He wrote to her parents on 18.3.26: 'Elfrida did thoroughbred work right from the start. It is no wonder she has got on. Her lessons have always been a pleasure to me and I am more than satisfied with what she has done in the time.'

She managed to fit in one more concert before her wedding – a song recital in Liverpool's Rushworth Hall on 2 March.

CHAPTER 4

Family Life

AFTER THESE concerts, Elfrida's musical career was put on hold and preparations for the wedding took priority. Dorothy and Edward held two 'At Homes' (on 16 and 17 April) which gave all their Manchester friends an opportunity to meet the couple and to bring wedding presents. There was also much to do to prepare their future home which was 10 Anson Road, a good-sized three-storey house in Victoria Park with a garden that backed on to the Dalton Hall grounds. Elfrida and Percy were married on the 21St April 1926 at Mount Street Friends Meeting House in central Manchester and afterwards they honeymooned in Corsica.

Elfrida and Percy's wedding

Although Elfrida carried out some previously arranged BBC schools transmissions on the history of song, she undertook no further concert engagements for about two years. She needed time to settle into married life and she also enjoyed family events such as her brother Cedric's marriage to Mary Adams (one of her school friends from The Mount) which took place in

10 Anson Road, Victoria Park

Northamptonshire in October 1926. Cedric and Mary then took over Surrey Lodge, the family home, and Edward and Dorothy moved into a house in Scarsdale Road, Victoria Park.

Elfrida also began to take a more active part in Quaker life in Manchester at that time. Two series of talks were arranged that year – 'What is Quakerism' and 'Quakerism and everyday life'. Elfrida spoke on 'Sacraments of the Church' in the first series and on 'Music' in the second.

Percy and Elfrida's first child, Robin Mary Vipont Foulds, was born on 2.6.27. Elfrida kept an account of the first actions and words of Robin and also noted her own feelings – 'I wish I could paint. The warm brown limbs are so disposed as if she had been in the act of turning when caught by slumber.' Singing lullabies was a very pleasant way of keeping in practise. Augustus Milner had hoped for something a little more structured and serious.

Since 1919, Percy had been working in the research department of Tootal Broadhurst Lee, a cotton manufacturing firm in Manchester. His research achievements had earned him the Fellowship of the Institute of Chemistry in 1924 and of the Textile Institute in 1925 and Tootals thought very highly of him.

The firm had continuing business in Italy and Percy was given the job of calling at offices in Milan or Venice to talk with Tootals' Italian colleagues and, if necessary, sort out problems. Elfrida often accompanied him on these journeys. In 1928 Elfrida wrote home enthusiastically – 'Pompeii far exceeded our expectations – Vesuvius was very angry – from the moment of our arrival Palermo delighted us – Girgenti is a dream of a place' and so on. They also travelled there twice in 1930.

Elfrida had not abandoned her singing career entirely and she still went up to London for lessons from time to time. She began to put together a programme of lecture recitals as she received many invitations to appear at charity occasions. Augustus Milner did not approve. In July 1928 she gave a recital in aid of the Women's International League for Peace and Freedom (WILPF) in the Lancashire College, Whalley Range, Manchester. In January 1929 she sang at a concert in Mount Street Meeting House for the Friends Guild of Teachers Conference. Her father (President of the Guild) was the main speaker. She had an excellent write-up in *The Friend* after this last concert –

> A wholly delightful song recital was given by Elfrida Vipont. Gifted with a beautiful soprano voice, Elfrida nevertheless charmed us principally by her interpretation. The singer lived in the spirit of the song, and showing insight and understanding held her audience spellbound to the last vibration of the last note.

Four months later, on 21 May, she gave birth to her second daughter – Carolyn Curtis.

Later in the year, in November, to celebrate Armistice Day, she gave another song recital in aid of the WILPF accompanied by Margaret Wills.

Elfrida enjoyed her singing, but she also enjoyed being at home with her growing family. It looked as if a full-time career as a singer was going to be difficult to fit in with family commitments at that time. Her thoughts turned to the possibility of writing a book that would combine both her musical and her historical interests. She realised she had material left over from her BBC broadcasts and from the lecture recitals and she was encouraged by the fact that she had been able to get articles published fairly easily. In

Lecture-Recitals

"EVERYONE SANG." (Some observations on the history of song in Europe.)
"PATINES OF BRIGHT GOLD." (A study of music at the French court, 1515–1715.)
"SHAKESPEARE'S SONGS."
"A PAGEANT OF ENGLISH OPERA."
"PASTIME WITH GOOD COMPANY." (Music at the English Court under the Tudors.)
"A SPORT OF KINGS." (Music at the English Court under the Stuarts.)
"FROM A PEAK IN DARIEN." (An introduction to the German Lieder writers.)
"SCHUBERT AND SONG."

Lantern Lecture-Recitals

(Travel talks illustrated by lantern slides and unaccompanied folk songs.)
"A STREET OF MANY HOUSES." (Musical Wayfaring in many lands.)
"TRAVEL AND SONG IN ITALY."

Story-Recitals

"DEAR SON OF MEMORY, GREAT HEIR OF FAME." (A summer's dream of the Boy Shakespeare.)
"THE BEAUTIFUL PURCELL."
"THE KING'S MUSICKE." (A pageant of Royal minstreisy.)
"COMMONWEAL." (An impression of music in England under the Commonwealth.)
"THE VOICE OF LYDEARD REGIS." (A vision of the golden age of English music.)
"OUR HERITAGE THE SEA." (English music goes a-roving.)
and other titles.

THESE LECTURES are all accompanied by vocal illustrations. The Lecture-Recitals take from an hour to an hour-and-a-quarter, whilst the Story-Recitals, suitable for younger audiences, take from twenty minutes to half-an-hour. Two of these last can be combined, if necessary, to give a full programme. Further particulars and terms can be obtained from

ELFRIDA VIPONT
10 ANSON ROAD
VICTORIA PARK
MANCHESTER

1929 she wrote *Good Adventure* – a story of music through the ages. Unfortunately, the first few publishers she approached sent the manuscript back to her as, in their opinion, they would not be able to sell enough copies for it to be profitable. Eventually, three years later, John Heywood Ltd was persuaded to publish it. The *Manchester Guardian* reviewer said, 'Miss Vipont essays a task beset with difficulties, some of which we think she has scarcely realised'. However, he did admit that her historical facts were sound. *The Friend* was more enthusiastic, but the book never became a best-seller.

In the meantime, Elfrida had been asked to contribute two chapters to a small book produced to celebrate the centenary of Mount Street Meeting House. This was published in 1930 and was on sale at the Centenary Celebrations. She also used her artistic talents and drew some of the 'tailpieces' at the ends of the chapters, but used the pseudonym 'Elizabeth Oldbridge'[6] for these. The celebrations were held from 22 to 26 October; her mother presided and both Elfrida and her father were among the speakers.

The discussion about Quakerism and the Arts was still a live issue in the pages of *The Friend* and Elfrida contributed two letters to this in 1929, writing that 'To my mind religion and art are inseparable' and 'A work of art is the outward and visible sign of an inner aesthetic experience.'

She still continued to have occasional singing lessons and also to give charitable song recitals. Augustus Milner did not, of course, approve of these as they did not fit in with his plans for her professional future career. He wanted her to spend more time in London so he could spend more time on her lessons. It was agonisingly difficult for Elfrida to decide on her priorities and in 1930 she wrote to him:

> It is out of the question to come up to London for a month on end or a week in every month. Nor can I sacrifice my writing or my children, or my Quaker principles for the sake of my singing. If I had to give up everything that makes life worth living in order to sing, I shouldn't have anything to

---

6. Vipont = Veteripont (Norman French origin) = old bridge.

say when I did sing. Singing and writing and all the rest of it can be combined into something which is worth doing, and worth working for, and worth living for and that something won't be a conventional recital career.

She gave another lecture recital in January 1931 – this time at her home (10 Anson Road). The programme was one she was to give on a number of future occasions: *'Some Aspects of Music at the French Court 1515-1715'*. Carl Fuchs (cellist with the Hallé and member of the Brodsky Quartet) and both John and Margaret Wills also took part. Elfrida sang two groups of songs.

Then, quite unexpectedly, another opportunity opened up. Elfrida was introduced to Elena Gerhardt, an established singer with an international reputation. Having heard Elfrida sing, she asked if a visit to Leipzig would be possible for a few weeks' tuition.

Soon afterwards Elfrida wrote again to Augustus Milner – a letter that virtually ended her time with him.

I'm afraid there's not much chance of my turning up at the studio for a bit. For one thing I'm doing a good deal of lecture recital work and I know that means 'No admittance'. For another this year's worse than last so far as cotton is concerned. Dad and Mother have just offered me a great opportunity. I met Gerhardt some time ago, and she asked if there was any chance of my going out to her for 3 or 4 weeks. I didn't think there was much but D & M promptly came to the rescue, so it looks as if I shall be going to Leipzig for three weeks some time this Spring.

The visit to Leipzig was quickly arranged and she was there from 10 to 25 April. Her mother went with her and wrote enthusiastically about the sightseeing, the concerts and Elfrida's lessons.

Gerhardt sang superbly in the concert last night. Opera begins at 6.0 so everyone rushes out and has a meal in the first interval. Elf's lesson is at 5.30 each day and is very strenuous. Gerhardt insists Elf knows the meaning of the words she sings. Elf is going to ask if she can have a lesson or two in London in June.

It was the Centenary of The Mount School that summer and Elfrida tried her hand at composing a new school song. She wrote both the words and the music of *'Fidelis in Parvo'* and they were ready in time for the annual Whitsuntide gathering of Old Scholars. Although an interesting change, the song was not taken up and substituted for the traditional school song.

The rest of 1931 and the beginning of 1932 saw a number of lecture recitals – in London's Grotian Hall *(Shakespeare's Songs)*, Manchester's Memorial Hall *(Pageant of English Opera)*, at Stramongate School, Kendal, in Ainsdale, and twice in Liverpool.

She had a much more major role to play in March 1932 when she sang the part of the angel in Elgar's *Dream of Gerontius* with the Wallasey Philharmonic Society. The reviews were good – 'She has an expressive voice which she uses well though a little lacking in repose for the Angel's music. There is a quiet sincerity about her work.'

This was followed by a concert in Manchester's Memorial Hall to celebrate the Haydn Bicentenary. Elfrida contributed three songs to this concert and although the *City News* thought that she 'sang sympathetically though we have heard her in better voice', the *Manchester Guardian* thought she had 'much improved since we last heard her.'

In the summer of 1932 the family paid a first visit to Yealand Conyers – the village near Carnforth in North Lancashire that was later to be their home. Elfrida was invited by Elisabeth Brockbank to speak to the

Elfrida with Robin and Carol at the seaside

38

Yealand Fellowship. They stayed in the Guest Cottage belonging to the Quaker Meeting and were so attracted by Yealand that they then came twice a year until war broke out. They enjoyed outings to the surrounding coast and to the Lake District.

Dorothy Croasdale was born on 25.11.32 and although Elfrida now had three small girls to look after, she was soon back on the lecture and recital trail. She spoke to Blackpool Quakers the following April on *'Music and Religion'* – the *Blackpool Times* said it was 'a truly thoughtful lecture and one that it was a pleasure to hear'. She wrote again to *The Friend* on much the same subject:

> Who can deny the sacramental significance of such music? Who can deny the sacramental significance of the Parthenon, York Minster, Chartres, Rodin's Le Penseur, Michelangelo's David, Mozart's Operas and Schubert's songs .....

Concerts in Manchester and Liverpool, both with much the same programme, were given in November and she received particularly good reviews. The *Manchester Guardian* noted that

> Since we last heard her sing Miss Vipont has cultivated a much more gracious lyrical utterance and she now sings through long legato lines with a breath control that keeps her tone smooth and her phrases well-nourished in their final notes.

She ended 1933 with a song recital in aid of the YWCA.[7]

In March 1934 she again shared a platform with Carl Fuchs in the German Church in Liverpool. Her reviews were very encouraging – 'Miss Vipont's Bach was a special joy, and the first two arias which she sang for her first group had a fine elation. It was delightful singing'. In May she gave a lecture recital on *Shakespeare's Songs* in Manchester's Memorial Hall. She was disappointed in the size of the audience and the reviewer did not think she had sufficient versatility of style or range of vocal colour. Later in the year she was again in the Memorial Hall and this time was much appreciated by the reviewer – 'Miss Vipont is clear and apt in her diction and the phrasing, especially in the

---

7. Young Womens Christian Association.

more subtle passages of Lieder, is thoroughly artistic.'

1934 also saw the publication of Elfrida's first really successful book – *Colin Writes to Friends House,* a book for teenagers about Quakerism, illustrated by Elisabeth Brockbank. 1500 copies were printed at first but these were soon sold and a second edition printed. Later, in 1957, there was a revised third edition. The book got rave reviews in the Quaker press and was welcomed particularly by children's committees. 'In writing this book Elfrida Vipont has supplied a long-felt need amongst Friends for an account of Quakerism for boys and girls. The account, in simple and unconventional style, is woven into a story of three children whose curiosity about Friends is roused and who write to Friends House for information.' *(The Wayfarer)* 'This is certainly a splendid book to give to young people at the enquiring age.' *(The Friend).* The *Church of England Newspaper* 'strongly recommended it for school libraries'.

However, Elfrida learnt a hard financial lesson. Friends Literature Committee paid £35 for the book and this was meant to include a payment to Elisabeth Brockbank – it barely covered their expenses. The Committee got a good bargain as it was a one-off payment and no royalties were included in the contract. No further payment to Elfrida was made when the second edition was printed, but she negotiated a 10% royalty on the third edition as that had been substantially revised by her. She did not make the same mistake again and always insisted on royalties in her book contracts.

Elfrida still continued to give lectures and lecture recitals. She sang in Welwyn Garden City in February 1935.

The birth of Ann Vipont on 5.9.1935 completed their family, but Elfrida was soon in the public eye again. She spoke on *'Music and Religion'* to Friends in Wilmslow Meeting in March 1936 and, also in March, gave her *'Music at the French Court'* lecture recital in the Memorial Hall (Manchester) which was very well received.

1936 was the year Elfrida was first appointed to serve on Ackworth School Committee, and this was the beginning of many years' service on a wide variety of Quaker committees.

1938 saw the publication of *Lift up your Lamps*. Elfrida had written this play to be performed during Mount Street Centenary celebrations and it was decided to publish it in 1938 in the hope that it would raise money to build a Meeting House for Wythenshawe (also in Manchester) Friends. It is a pageant about the history of Manchester Friends and is written to be performed by the children of the Meeting. The little book received good reviews from the Quaker press – 'If only all Friends' Meetings with ancient records would produce a Pageant of this nature. It is a capital way to arouse interest in our history and beliefs'. Elfrida composed a song (words and music) to be performed with the pageant.

Elfrida finished another book, *Blow the Man Down*, in 1938 although it was not finally published until 1939. The Friends Literature Committee were not sure whether this was the sort of book they wanted to back – an adventure story – even though it was based on a true Quaker story. Elfrida tried the Oxford University Press (OUP) but they asked her to use a male name as this was a boys' story. Reluctantly she complied and became 'Charles Vipont'. Afterwards, Kathleen Lines from the OUP wrote to her – 'I would like to congratulate you on a superb piece of work'.

CHAPTER 5

World War II

ELFRIDA AND her children spent the whole of the Second World War at Yealand Conyers in North Lancashire where she was headmistress of the evacuation school at Yealand Manor.[8] In 1938 the Government evacuated some children from the big cities, thinking that war was imminent, but then, due to the Munich agreement which postponed hostilities, they were returned home. The evacuation had been chaotic – particularly since arrangements for the children's education had been less

Yealand Manor

---

8. Full details can be found in The Story of Yealand Manor School by Susan V. Harshorne.

than adequate. Elfrida and two other Manchester Quakers (Margery Wilson and Christine Sutherland) decided they wanted something better for their children. Quakers already had a number of secondary schools situated well away from potential bombing; so the need was for elementary/primary school education. They knew about the Quaker guesthouse and conference centre at Yealand Manor and planned to establish a temporary school there for the duration of the war and to use volunteers to staff the school. They brought their plans to the Overseers at Mount Street Meeting who were glad to endorse their ideas. No-one, of course, thought the war would last as long as it did.

In total, about 180 children passed through the school and almost all remember it with affection as a very happy place. Anthony Wilson notes that, 'Of the six schools and two universities which I have attended, I count Yealand as providing the best learning environment and the happiest community of pupils and teachers.'

Most of the children came from the badly bombed northern cities (Manchester, Liverpool and Leeds) but there were a few from the south of England and some were refugees from war-torn Europe: there were 15 refugees from 6 countries. Some children came with their mothers and their mothers were incorporated into the staff. Others arrived in the UK on Kindertransport on their own, or had been interned before coming to Yealand. Many had had horrific experiences and took some time to adjust. In one report, Elfrida said

> The dark haired little Czech girl who was quite clearly going to be brilliant (she won a scholarship to secondary school when she was only nine) had very loving kindly foster parents who cared for her very tenderly. But in class she needed much reassurance, feeling conscious of the language difficulty, and of the many subtle little ways in which she was different from these English children – she, for example, didn't know their weights and measures, and used a different style of writing. And out on walks she always wanted to hold the grownup's hand.

This little girl (Renata (Polger) Laxova) came to Britain on Kindertransport and had left both her parents behind.

Pupils at the school

It was not an easy time for Elfrida. She was full of enthusiasm at first and hoped not only to provide a safe place for the children, but also to conduct an educational and social experiment which would be the testing house for, as she said 'new ideas capable of revolutionising and revitalising our national and international life'. However, many of the children were homesick as they had not been away from home before without their parents and at first there was an acute shortage of equipment. The refugee children needed, not surprisingly, extra attention and it also took some time for them to acquire ration books. Fortunately some of her volunteer staff had teaching experience and qualifications but many did not – and neither did she! Some of her staff were young men who had registered as conscientious objectors to military service and were summoned (often at very short notice) to Tribunal Hearings and they were sometimes imprisoned. It was difficult to weld all these diverse elements into a community.

Nevertheless, and in spite of the difficulties, over the course of the school's existence 27 scholarships and/or exhibitions were obtained – mainly to Friends Schools – and the school passed inspections by HMIs and others with flying colours. In April 1944 the HMI's report said:

The school work is planned on sound lines, approximating very closely to, and indeed in some ways going a little further than, the work done by children of these ages in a public elementary school. ... There is a family spirit in the school. The various forms are small in number and thus every opportunity is afforded for close attention to individual needs and the children make progress at their own pace. It can confidently be said at the outset that the children are receiving sound instruction and that, in general, their attainments are very creditable. ... They have acquired a good command of language and are able to talk about their work with ease.

Elfrida's own musical training as a singer had made her aware of how valuable it would be if music could be introduced as an integral part of the curriculum. She introduced regular 'Listening Times' in which the children were taught to sit quietly and listen to music – at first to very short items and then, later, when they had got used to this discipline, to whole programmes. One mother wrote, describing her first visit to the school:

I heard music in one of the rooms. Some of the parents had started to play a trio by Mendelssohn. Some small children came on tiptoes into this room and listened silently. I wondered who had taught them to be full of respect and awe before beauty.

Then, in the summer of 1940, a letter came from Arthur and Winifred Percival offering their services to the school. Arthur played violin in the Hallé orchestra (later he became deputy leader) and Winnie was a concert pianist. They came to Yealand in September, stayed until the school closed and took charge of music, achieving miracles and giving many of the children an interest in music that lasted all their lives.

They worked on the principle that every child could be taught some instrument – even if they never progressed beyond banging an improvised drum. Somehow or other instruments were found. A violin and a recorder were given by the Hallé; bamboo pipes were made in craft lessons; Percy Foulds managed to acquire a bass drum and cymbals; some other percussion instruments were received from a friend; and parents, friends and visitors lent a variety of violins, a cello and a flute. Gradually an orchestra was formed. Winnie Percival wrote:

> Arthur must have spent hundreds of hours writing and arranging and composing and simplifying orchestral parts. Every child had a part it could read, and really enjoy playing at that particular moment. If, after its next lesson, it could manage something more advanced, at the next rehearsal it was presented with a more difficult part, and played it – very often before the ink was dry!

The orchestra gave a number of local concerts and once went to Manchester to perform in Mount Street Meeting House.

There was also a strong emphasis on the value of art, crafts and drama in the school. Art classes were taken by Margery Wilson who was also a keen naturalist and introduced the city children to the treasures of the countryside. Regular school plays were performed for the local villagers and most of the children took part.

Elfrida wrote about religious education in the school (in an unpublished account):

Yealand Children's orchestra

From the very first, religious education was thought to be the centre of life at Yealand. Actually it formed the basis of the concern from which the whole work sprang.... Yealand was envisaged as a place where as many children as possible might be gathered together during the war years and trained, however imperfectly, to live in that spirit 'which takes away the occasion of all wars'.

Each day began with School Assembly which was attended by all the children. A hymn was sung followed by a short period of silence. Elfrida herself taught Scripture throughout the school – from stories and Bible picture books for the very youngest to detailed work on the meaning of the Lord's Prayer to the oldest children. She felt that the most important thing in the Kindergarten classes was that the children should enjoy their Scripture lessons and associate them with happiness. Later, when they were about seven, they were introduced to the Bible and given some idea of its contents – covering most of the well-known Old Testament stories. The following year they would be introduced to the New Testament and in the top form a course of lessons on the Lord's Prayer was always given. Special festivals (Christmas, Easter and Whitsuntide) were also worked into the lessons. Elfrida's talents as a storyteller flourished with the constant practice.

Sunday always ended with Evening Meeting at the school and there were hymns, often a reading, a talk or story and sometimes a prayer. Often visiting Friends, or anyone else Elfrida thought would be interesting, gave the talk. Sometime sthe talk was replaced with some music played by the Percivals or visiting musicians.

Sadly Elfrida put so much into the school that her health suffered. The Testimony that was written after her death said:

> Elfrida drove her body beyond its capabilities and with the closure of the School in the autumn of 1944 she suffered a severe breakdown. She was occasionally to be seen at that time in the corridors of Friends House, almost haggard in appearance and making her way slowly with a stick.

Fortunately she soon recovered and in a number of the children's books she wrote subsequently it is possible to see glimpses of her Yealand Manor School experiences. She had learnt a lot about the needs and reactions of children who came from very different backgrounds to her own.

If the war years were not easy for Elfrida, neither were they easy for her family. They all lived in the Guest Cottage near the Meeting House which was cramped compared with their house in Manchester and which was also often used to provide accommodation for other children. Robin was already at Ackworth when the war began and Carol soon joined her. They were both later to transfer to The Mount School in York. However, Dudy (Dorothy) and Ann were at Yealand for the whole time and did not always enjoy having to share their mother with all those extra children. Ann remembers staying up at the Manor long after most of the other children had gone to bed because Elfrida had work to finish – and their both being rescued by Percy when he came home after a long day in Manchester. When Robin and Carol came home for the holidays there were always tasks needing to be done at the school, and they remember working at cleaning in the kitchen every morning.

In 1944, when the end of the war was in sight, and many of the children were able to go home, the decision was made to close the school.

CHAPTER 6

Post War Changes

THE END of the war in 1945 brought great rejoicings, but there were also major decisions to be made for the Foulds family. Perhaps the most urgent question to be decided was whether to return to Manchester or to stay in Yealand. They had all grown fond of Yealand but if they were to stay in the village, somewhere had to be found to live as they could not continue to stay in the cottage.

Whether or not they decided to stay in Yealand, they had to clear their Manchester house (10 Anson Road) so that they could either sell or occupy it. They had let the house during the war and afterwards, not surprisingly, found that a considerable amount of repair work needed to be done.

It was eventually decided that they would stay in Yealand and that Percy would continue to commute to Manchester to work at Tootals. They bought and moved into Green Garth in 1945. This was a seventeenth century farmhouse in the village with a large garden. It was to be their home for the rest of their lives. A year later, Elfrida's father retired from general practice in Manchester at the age of 82 – having stayed on for the duration of the war as he was needed because most of the younger doctors had been conscripted into the armed forces. He and Dorothy sold their house in Scarsdale Road, left their son Cedric in charge of the practice, and joined the family at Green Garth. Edward did not take easily to retirement; adjustments had to be made; and the next few years were not easy for any of them.

Yealand Manor was then run as a guest house by Percy's sister Mary and her husband Burtt Meyer until it was sold to the Provincial Insurance Company in 1956.

Green Garth

By the time Edward and Dorothy moved to Green Garth, Robin was at Manchester University, and Carol and Dudy (Dorothy) were still at The Mount. Ann, however, was too young to go to The Mount so she spent two years at a school in Bolton-le-Sands before joining the others in York.

Elfrida didn't return to singing, but she soon took up her writing again. She was delighted to have a study to retire to and furnished it with floor to ceiling bookshelves. Percy enjoyed making things grow – both flowers and vegetables – and spent hours in the garden. They had the space now to add dogs to the family and thereafter there was a succession of small

Four daughters

dogs to be taken regularly for walks – Rufus the corgi was the first of several.

Elfrida soon started writing the first of what was to be her most successful series – the Lark books. *The Lark in the Morn* was published (by the Oxford University Press) in 1948 and is the story of Kit, a young girl who is at first misunderstood by her family but who eventually goes on to have a career as a singer. It was to be an immediate success and was reprinted three times. She had good reviews from both sides of the Atlantic. The *New York Times* said:

Elfrida with corgi, 1950s

> Mrs Vipont, a musician, has written a moving story of a young artist in the making. It is peopled with interesting characters, young and old, filled with the sense of music, and with the quiet wisdom of the Quaker way of life.

Some years later Elfrida had a letter asking questions about the book from a young fan, who said: 'I very much liked the way in which the books were written. I can't help wondering which parts (if any) were related to your own experiences? .... Which people in the stories were based, or drawn from, people you have actually met or known?' Elfrida answered:

> It isn't easy to answer your questions about which parts of the books are related to my own experiences, because on the one hand I think books grow out of the writer's inward experiences, but on the other hand, all the outward experiences in life go into the making of them. For instance, I'm a Quaker and I went to a Quaker boarding school, but Kit's experiences aren't my own.

A fellow author, Geoffrey Trease, said, encouragingly: 'May she produce a sequel to her magnificent *Lark in the Morn*'. She did.

The Lark on the Wing was soon in preparation, and this received even wider acclaim. She was awarded the Library Association's Carnegie Medal for the most outstanding book for children published during 1950. The medal was presented at the Annual Conference of the Association in Edinburgh and Elfrida's acceptance speech was much admired by the committee. One of them said: 'She summed up the purpose of the medal better than I have ever heard it described when she said that the point of an honour like this was that one had to go on earning it. I must never now,' she concluded, 'fall short of the standard you have set.' Requests for autographs, for sequels, for a story about a Quaker boy – all poured in. Later, in 1959, the Australian Broadcasting Association asked if they could do a dramatisation of the book.

It was not until 1957 that the next book in the Lark series – *The Spring of the Year* – was published. A young reader – Millie, from Jamaica – wrote to Elfrida saying 'I like the story of Laura best. I hope you will write one of when she grows up'. Millie had to wait until 1960 before she could read *Flowering Spring*. And the last of the Lark books, *The Pavilion*, was not published until 1969. They were all popular though the later books never achieved the same commercial success as the first two. However, by the time the last book was published, the tangled web of

The author at work

relationships over several generations had got so complicated that some readers had difficulty in remembering who was related to who – in spite of Elfrida's helpful family tree.

As well as *The Lark on the Wing*, Elfrida produced another successful book, *Sparks Among the Stubble*, in 1950. This was a book of stories – several with Quaker connections – that she had told over and over again to the children at Yealand Manor School. *The Times Educational Supplement* said: 'Miss Vipont is a born story-teller who can thrill or uplift without a single unreal stroke.' And Caroline Graveson, a notable educationalist and renowned for her gifts as a story-teller, wrote:

> I found myself reading it straight through heedless of other duties. There are some children's books – the best of them, I believe – which appeal almost as much to older people; their directness, clear motivation and absence of 'cleverness' are so genuinely refreshing.

Elfrida was delighted when, in January 1951, her daughter Carol married Richard (Rikki) Robson. Their daughter Cressida was born in the following November. Another joyful occasion took place when Robin married Kenneth Greaves in July of the same year. Kenneth was appointed to a post at Sidcot Quaker School in 1952.

Family group – including the two new sons-in-law

At about this time Elfrida had a number of relatively minor health problems. She fell down the front door steps and injured her back and she also suffered from sciatica. However, she refused to be treated as an invalid – though she did agree to some physiotherapy – and insisted on carrying on as usual. This stoical approach was perhaps helped by the need to prepare for the Quaker Tercentenary celebrations in 1952 – an event she was anticipating with pleasure. She also continued to relish the letters sent by enthusiastic fans who had enjoyed *Lark in the Morn* and *Sparks among the Stubble*.

1952 started well. The BBC was interested in her *'Cream of Paradise'* story from *Sparks among the Stubble* and wanted to broadcast this in their run of programmes: *'Adventures in English'*. Elfrida accepted their offer and successfully resisted their attempts to make unwelcome alterations. Later they approached her again and asked her to do the dramatisation of two of the other stories in *Sparks among the Stubble* – *'Things that go bump in the night'* and *'John Crook, Quaker'*.

As clerk[9] of Yealand Meeting and also a member of the 1652 Committee, she was deeply involved in organising the week-long celebrations in the north-west to mark the Tercentenary of the foundation of the Society of Friends. Cumbria will always have a special place in the hearts of Quakers because it was to Margaret Fell's home at Swarthmoor Hall in Ulverston that George Fox, the founder of Quakerism, made his way in 1652. He later married the recently widowed Margaret Fell. It was from Swarthmoor Hall that the so-called 'Valiant Sixty' set out to preach Quakerism in all parts of the UK and also in many corners of the world. So it has become a place of pilgrimage to which groups of Quakers come to learn about their history. They come from Quaker Meetings, from Quaker Schools, from Woodbrooke Quaker College in Birmingham, and from Quaker Colleges and Meetings in other parts of the world.

Elfrida gave the address in Lancaster Town Hall which brought to an end the Tercentenary Celebrations. She was not

---

9. This is an administrative Quaker post combining the duties of secretary and chair.

Yealand Friends Meeting House

only concerned with the past, however, but with inspiring Friends to look to the future, and she said:

> We have been together for a very memorable week. Do we take back with us memories of things that happened three hundred years ago? If we only take back such memories, then it may be that we have had a vision of a valley of dry bones, and the bones will be very dry. God forbid! Not while we live! 'Come from the four winds, O breath, and breathe upon these slain, that they may live in us.'

Those who knew Elfrida will be very familiar with this quotation from Ezekiel's 'valley of dry bones' (Chapter 37). It was often in her mind and was referred to in a number of talks she gave.

After the Tercentenary Celebrations the 1652 Committee continued to arrange visits to Cumbria, and later Elfrida took over the clerkship of that committee. Many remember how inspiring she was when she spoke of the lives of 17th century Quakers. On one of the Schools Pilgrimages, Joyce Pickard remembers Elfrida's ringing voice: 'Stand for truth, John, stand for truth!'

She can still hear that voice and has never forgotten that challenge. Howard Brunton writes of another similar occasion:

> We stayed at Yealand where we were cared for by Elfrida. My most powerful memory was on our visit to Brigflatts Meeting House where she ministered both historically and spiritually. Enhanced by the environment, it was a moving experience.

Chris and Christina Lawson led many groups from Woodbrooke to the 1652 country in the years from 1970 to 1992 and remember the warm welcome Elfrida gave them

> Elfrida's welcome was always 'We get many pilgrimage groups but the Woodbrooke one is always special'. Maybe she said that to all the other groups too, but we did produce a dozen nationalities from 20 people sometimes. We'd introduce ourselves and there'd be singing and talking through the evening. Sometimes Elfrida would be persuaded to sing and we'd be held spellbound by her musical gifts.
>
> Vital to the experience for the groups was encountering Elfrida, drawn by her warmth, brightness of eye, interest in everyone and captivated by her story telling. These were not long-gone people of whom she spoke but ones that lived within her still. She really wanted to tell us about them.

Elfrida and corgi, 1960s

Occasionally, the Lawsons said, her passion for story-telling spilled over into her talks and

> Historical precision at times may have given way to making them real through little details of their lives which could be presumed and which would hold the attention of any touring group, young or old.

They remember particularly visits to Camsgill and Elfrida's

assertion that 'The road to Pennsylvania begins here' (see p.69); her ability to bring the Fell family to life to the groups visiting Swarthmoor Hall; and talking about Margaret Fell in Yealand Meeting House. They recall that even in her last years, when she was brought over to the Meeting House in a wheelchair, she still had power to challenge her audience so that 'We knew we had been in the presence of one through whom Quaker testimony past and present fused together'.

Adrian Smith recalls how Elfrida played a part in his becoming a Quaker. First, by speaking at his Quarterly Meeting in Colchester and then the next year when he went on a Pilgrimage to the 1652 country he was shown round by Elfrida who gave a very full commentary. He says: 'To see the actual spots where key events in the start of Quakerism occurred, suddenly made it all drop into place'

As part of the Tercentenary Celebrations and for continuing use by Quakers, Elfrida produced *'The Birthplace of Quakerism – A Handbook for the 1652* Country' – a guide to the places held to be important to Quakers in Cumbria. Bernard Canter said (reviewing it in *The Friend*) that it was 'one of the most attractive publications issued from Friends House of recent years.' A revised copy of this guide is still in use and helping to revise it was almost the last task she was able to do for Friends. She served for very many years on the 1652 Committee, and eventually handed over to Margery Wilson. In the mid-1970s a set of slides was made to illustrate talks on the 1652 country and Elfrida was able to take these with her on her later trips to visit US Quakers.

It is not surprising also to find her name on the list of members of the Swarthmoor Hall Committee - a committee that looked after the fabric of this historic building as well as the visitors who flocked to see it. She served on this committee from 1951 to 1977. Margaret Fell was one of Elfrida's heroines and she wrote a number of articles about her and often referred to her in the talks she gave. *'A Lily Among Thorns'* (a booklet about Margaret Fell) was also published in 1952.

CHAPTER 7

An Almost Full-time Author

AT THE end of 1952 and during much of 1953 Elfrida's back problems caught up with her. An X-ray confirmed that she had ruptured a disc and prolonged rest was prescribed. She did not enjoy this! It had been suggested some time previously that she might write a history of Quakerism that would be suitable for teenagers and for those new to Quakerism. She had been working on this for some time and was nearing the end. So she found the hours she had to spend on her back most frustrating as she was unable to get to her typewriter. Mary Milligan was enlisted to type the final version of *The Story of Quakerism* and at last it was finished. Then followed a search for a publisher, but this did not prove to be easy. The Oxford University Press turned it down – they said they were not familiar with the market for that sort of publication as it did not 'fit in very well with a University Press list'. Eventually it was published by the Bannisdale Press in 1954. In a glowing review in *The Friend*, Mary Hooper (Head of Sidcot Friends School) said: 'Generations of Scripture teachers in Friends Schools will rise up and call the author blessed.' It was deservedly popular and was reprinted in 1955 and again in 1959. Quaker schools and meetings bought it for their libraries and to give to their teenagers.

In spite of her back problems, Elfrida continued to write articles (one for an American periodical, *The Intelligencer*, about Yealand Christmases 12.12.53) and reviews (of Janet Whitney's *'Elizabeth Fry: Quaker Heroine'*) and to give talks (for example, to children in Preston Library *23.10.53*).

The next few years saw personal tragedy strike Elfrida's family. Early in 1954 Percy died. He had been ill for some time with emphysema and his lungs gradually wore out. He had recently been appointed President of Ackworth Old Scholars Association – a post he was delighted to accept – and had already written his presidential address. Sadly he did not live to deliver it. Elfrida sent it to the school and extracts were read by Rex Yates. Percy had been Elfrida's firm foundation – keeping her feet on the ground when she set herself unachievable goals; being there for the family when headmistress Elfrida ran out of time; helping to sort out financial problems; and always able to bring laughter into the house.

A year later, Elfrida's father died. He had grown up in a much more patriarchal society and had found the changes to society, largely brought about by WW2, difficult to accept. He had been a much loved and well respected family doctor, but had not been easy to look after during his final years when he himself needed medical and nursing attention.

Carol, Rikki and their daughter Cressida had by this time been in the Sudan for some time as Rikki was working there. In the spring of 1956 Elfrida received the horrific news that they had all been in a car accident. Rikki had died and Carol and Cressida had been hurt. Elfrida immediately went out to help Carol pack up and come back to England.

Edward and Dorothy

To add to Elfrida's difficulties, it had become clear that her income from writing was going to be essential in the future to enable her to stay in Green Garth. And write she did. For the rest of her life she continued to produce books for all ages on a wide variety of subjects.

After Percy's death, and when she had recovered sufficiently to start writing again, Elfrida realised that she really needed some secretarial assistance if the writing business was to be taken seriously. Up until then she had typed all her manuscripts herself and, although she managed adequately when producing short articles, it took her a long time to finish a whole book - time which she was sure could be spent more creatively. She advertised for someone who could take the position on a permanent basis. Elizabeth Morris - always known as Betty - answered the advert and stayed with Elfrida for the next twenty years. Not only did she type the manuscripts, articles and letters but she also managed the house, cooked meals and proved a loving and devoted companion to Elfrida's mother in her old age - leaving Elfrida time and space to do the things she really wanted to do. Betty Morris lived at Milnthorpe which was near enough (about 8 miles away) so that she could go home at weekends. She became a friend of the family and everyone missed her when she retired in the mid- 70s. However she was persuaded in 1978 to return and work part time – for two mornings a week.

In 1955 Elfrida published another book for boys, *The Heir of Craigs* – again under the name of 'Charles Vipont'. This was an adventure story which was enjoyed by many teenagers and by Hugh Barbour who said 'I was surprised and eventually delighted by the unusual ending, as well as by familiar names like Witherslack Hall.' However, although the Oxford University Press tried to sell this in the USA they were told it was too gloomy to appeal to that market.

1955 also saw the first of the Dowbiggins books – *The Family at Dowbiggins*. This had mixed reviews. *The Times Literary Supplement* (TLS) said it was 'competent and enjoyable but does not bear comparison with her earlier work – a disappointing book by a fine author.' The *Friends Journal* on 17.12.55 wrote that it was 'wholesome but exciting' – slightly better! And the *British Book News* in February 1956 thought it a 'comfortable family chronicle'. Later Elfrida wrote sequels – *More about Dowbiggins* (1958) and *Changes at Dowbiggins* (1960) but the TLS was still not convinced.

Her biography of Arnold Rowntree – also published in 1955 – was, on the other hand, very favourably received. Ian Hyde, writing in *The Friend* (1.12.55), said 'Elfrida Vipont has kept strictly and honestly to writing the 'life course of a human being' and in doing so she has given us a vivid portrait of a warm-hearted outreaching personality.' Mary Rowntree (Arnold's widow) wrote to Elfrida on 20.2.56 telling her that she had had 'such warm letters of appreciation from many who have enjoyed it and that has been so cheering'. One such letter said that Elfrida had made Arnold Rowntree 'live again in his gracious, kindly characteristic way in our hearts and memories again.' Not only was this cheering to Mary Rowntree, but also to Elfrida.

The Times Literary Supplement was much better pleased with the Christian anthology Elfrida wrote for teenagers which was published just before Christmas 1957. It said, '*The High Way* is wholly admirable. It is by far the best value of all books mentioned in this review and can be recommended without reserve'. The Mother's Union also recommended it as an idea for a Christmas present, and several school heads enthused about its use in school assemblies. Ian Hyde in *The Friend* (29.11.57) thought that although it was written with teenagers in mind, it spoke to all grown-ups as well.

Seeing the success of *The High Way*, Collins wrote and asked Elfrida if she would compile an anthology for younger children. *Bless This Day* was welcomed by *The Times Educational Supplement* and their critic noted it was 'an imaginative anthology of prayers for children set in peaceful and reflective coloured drawings by Harold Jones'. Again this caught the Christmas market and many journals recommended it as a suitable present. It was on Godfrey Winn's Christmas list in *The Church Times* (28.11.58) and he said, 'This collection is of true value and will enrich the spiritual life of countless children both now and as they grow up.' The book sold well and was still popular in the 1980s.

The next twenty-five years saw the production of a large number of books on a wide variety of subjects. Elfrida managed to combine this with international travel (described in the next chapter), writing numerous articles, responding to requests to give talks, playing an active part in both her local Quaker Meeting and in national Quaker work and, not least, taking part in a number of family matters.

Henry Purcell and his Times was published in 1959 to catch

Purcell's Tercentenary celebrations and was well received by both the literary press and by schools. *British Book News* reported 'it can be recommended to teachers and parents who wish to rouse children's interest in Purcell's music'. Although the *Manchester Guardian* didn't care for it and thought it a 'mishmash of historical "colour" writing', *Music* and *Musicians* found it excellent and 'interestingly written'. Kathleen Carrick Smith, Head of The Mount School, wrote to Elfrida, saying that she 'admired the skill with which you put him into his historical setting in such a lively and attractive way' and that the book 'should do a great deal to extend the present revival of his music to a younger generation.' Elfrida had greatly enjoyed researching and writing this book, combining as it did both her musical and historical interests. Later, in 1967, when she was commissioned by the Oxford University Press to write a book about Purcell for younger children (*Child of the Chapel Royal*) she was able to use much of the same research.

In the summer of 1968 Elfrida's mother, Dorothy Brown, died, gently and graciously as she had lived. In her last few days, as her great-grandchildren played in the garden outside her bedroom window, she took out her hearing-aid and said, 'Tell the children to make as much noise as they like. I shan't hear them.' She was much loved by all who knew her.

Elfrida's interest in religion went far beyond her Quaker background and practice - for much of her time at Yealand she regularly took part in a number of local church activities, for a time sang in the church choir and occasionally was known to have played the organ. And research for several books published in the early 60s deepened and expanded her knowledge. The first of these was *The Story of Christianity in Britain*. After some correspondence with the publishers, Michael Joseph, about illustrations which were not thought to be acceptable, this was published in 1960 and was welcomed not just by Quakers but by, among others, Methodists, Anglicans and the Bible Churchmen's Missionary Society. The Suffragan Bishop of Portsmouth wrote to Elfrida after he had read his complimentary copy:

> I am most grateful for this and am trying it out on my tenyear-old son, who obviously is enjoying it. I shall certainly do my best to commend it, and am most grateful to you for

sending it to me.

Then the next year saw the publication of *What about Religion?* This received complimentary remarks from both Quaker and non-Quaker teachers – Tom Green, Head of Bootham School said that in his opinion, 'it would meet a very real need'. Another anthology followed (*The Bridge*) in 1962 which was greeted by one reader as 'A very precious book – it will be a guide and inspiration to many' and has been as Ted Milligan said 'a magnificent quarry of material for many a person stuck for a reading at school assembly'. It was followed (in 1963) by *Some Christian Festivals* – a fascinating account of the origin and meaning of both well known and (to most people) obscure festivals.

In 1965 Elfrida wrote *Quakerism - A Faith to Live By*. Published by the Bannisdale Press, it was to become a Quaker best-seller on both sides of the Atlantic and she also used it as the basis for some of her lectures. An American Quaker, Tom Bodine, wrote:

> I am most impressed by the way you make the people come alive. This is a book about the main tenets of Quakerism: that no intermediaries are necessary between man and God; that there is something of God in every one; in that a man's faith must be something he lives by.

George Fox and the Valiant Sixty was published in 1975 and, this was also, as its name implies, aimed at the Quaker market and at first sold well. However, there are a lot of similar books available and five years later when the print run was finished, Hamish Hamilton did not advise a reprint.

These books with a religious theme were interspersed with two more of the Lark series: *Flowering Spring* (1960) and *The Pavilion* (1969); another in the Dowbiggins series: *Changes at Dowbiggins* (1960); and Search for a Song (1962). Then the first of a series of books for younger children – *The Offcomers* – was commissioned by Hamish Hamilton and published in 1965. This was followed over the years 1965-9, in the same series by *Larry Lopkins, Rescue for Mittens, Stevie, The Secret Passage, The China Dog* and *Michael and the Dogs*. The *Times Literary Supplement* was not exactly enthusiastic and said *Rescue for Mittens* (about a kitten) was 'a pleasant enough little story for the seven-year-olds, but lacking in any vitality, humour or imagination'. However, Elfrida's young readers seemed to like them, and they provided useful income for her. *Stevie* (about a dog) was illustrated by Raymond Briggs and was the start of a partnership that led to their extremely successful book for very young children, *The Elephant and the Bad Baby* - published in 1969 and still, at the time of writing, a best-seller and counted by many as a classic. It has had a number of reprints and has been translated into several languages.

Anyone who visited Elfrida's home at Green Garth would be told about the ghosts she believed she shared the house with. So it is not surprising that one of her books (*Terror by Night* 1966) is a compilation of ghost stories. She uses the device of the stories being told by and to the visitors to a music school at an old house. A 13 year old reader approved and wrote to Elfrida, saying, 'Having the stories told by the people at Thwaite How makes the stories become truer and more enthralling'. The book was reprinted by an American publisher in 1967 under the title of *Ghosts' High Noon*.

In 1974 *Bed in Hell* was published. Elfrida had for some time been fascinated by the story of Jane Stuart and her probable royal and also Quaker connections. She combined this theme with an adventure story featuring a murderous and cruel anti-hero who can never escape from his bitter childhood experiences and who makes his 'Bed in Hell'. As the review in *Quaker Monthly* said

> The elements of fact and fiction are subtly interwoven in this story, for Jane Stuart did exist, her death is recorded in the Chatteris (formerly Wisbech & Sutton) Monthly Meeting Register.

The review in *The Friend* was enthusiastic – 'The author writes with a true sense of history, a poetic imagination and a beautiful economy of words'

The Brontës, Jane Austen and George Eliot had formed some of Elfrida's early reading and as a young teenager she had copied the Brontës' habit of writing stories in tiny little booklets she had made herself. She didn't know a great deal about Charlotte Brontë's early life and was, no doubt, glad to be given the opportunity by John Day (US publishers) of increasing her knowledge. However, this was not a relationship that had a happy ending. When she had finished the manuscript, John Day wanted amendments and additions that Elfrida felt she could not agree to. The dispute lingered on and in the end the help of the Society of Authors was requested. It was eventually agreed that she should get the manuscript back and could seek another publisher. Hamish Hamilton published the book with the title *Weaver of Dreams: the girlhood of Charlotte Brontë* and it was a success. So much so that they asked her to write similar books on the early lives of George Eliot (*Towards a High Attic*) and Jane Austen *(A Little Bit of Ivory)*. She was particularly interested in this last book as an early ancestor of hers, William Curtis, had been Jane Austen's doctor and there is an unconfirmed rumour that Mr Perry's character (Mr Woodhouse's doctor in *Emma*) is based on William Curtis. So Elfrida was glad to have the opportunity to visit Alton while researching for her book. The Jane Austen Society welcomed the book and said, 'It is charmingly done and accurate and comprehensive.'

In among all these books, Elfrida also wrote short stories and articles on a wide variety of subjects. She wrote an article on music for the *Girl's Own Book of Hobbies*; one story in a book published by Blackwell's called '*Five More*'; an article entitled 'About a famous Writer' (Charles Dickens) and also 'Bruin the Guard' both for *Jack and Jill*; and 'The Show must go on' and 'The Light that never was' for Noel Streatfield's *Ballet Annual*.

Throughout this time, Elfrida's Quaker work also increased. Her work on the 1652 Committee and the Swarthmoor Hall Committee has already been mentioned. Serving as clerk of Yealand Meeting was at times an extension of this work as 1652 visitors usually stayed at Yealand. And before there were adequate kitchen facilities at the Meeting House, Green Garth was always available for cups of tea after Meeting on Sundays.

In addition to these local Quaker activities Elfrida was increasingly involved in national Quaker affairs. She represented Lancashire and Cheshire Quarterly Meeting on Meeting for Sufferings (*the Quaker national executive body*) for three periods (1938-42, 1945-59 and 1962-67). She was then appointed clerk and served in that capacity from 1969-74. Diana Lampen recalls that on Elfrida's birthday they all sang 'Happy Birthday' to her and she responded: 'I can think of no better way to spend my birthday than coming to Meeting for Sufferings!' This appointment did not only mean clerking the often complex monthly business meetings, but she also became involved in attending numerous subcommittees ex officio. She was in addition a member of the Book Centre Management Committee, the Library Committee, the Committee that revised *Christian Faith and Practice* - and many others!

In all of her committee work Elfrida is remembered as always being particularly well prepared and well able to grasp the ins and outs of often difficult situations. Staff members knew they had to be prepared for her searching questions. In spite of her diminutive stature Elfrida was well able to control the meetings she clerked and to help members find the right way forward. Ted Milligan said:

> Elfrida was never casual in her approach. She studied her agendas; her comments were shrewd, to the point and, in difficult situations, conciliatory. She never spoke overmuch; indeed, sometimes her fellow members wished she would speak more, for her opinion was valued, while her memory often put present troubles in a useful perspective.

And Diana Lampen remembers that her contributions were

Opening the swimming bath at The Mount as MOSA President, 1965

always 'robust and unfailingly helpful'.

Elfrida also had very close involvement with both The Mount School and with Ackworth School. She had been, of course, a pupil at The Mount and was delighted to be appointed (like her mother before her) President of The Mount Old Scholars Association in 1965/6. In that capacity she opened the new Swimming Baths and Sports Centre. She said that she swam whenever she had the opportunity and,

> I have swum in a wide variety of places in my life.....in the North Sea, the Irish Sea, the Channel, the Atlantic Ocean, the Pacific, the Tasman Sea, the Great Lakes - and Bootham School swimming bath.'

Until these new baths were opened, the girls had to walk across York to Bootham School whenever they needed to swim.

Her love for Ackworth began with her love for Percy who had been a pupil there and who was always very enthusiastic in his praise of the school and who sadly died before he could take up his position as President of the Old Scholars Association. They sent two of their girls (Robin and Carol) to the school (they both later went on to The Mount) and it gave Elfrida great pleasure to discover that some of her ancestors had been among the early pupils at Ackworth. She served for many years on the school committee and was delighted to find that committee members were eligible for membership of Ackworth Old Scholars Association. She took out membership immediately and in due course became president of that body also. In 1959 she wrote a history of Ackworth School.

Elfrida was a long standing member of the Friends Historical Society (FHS). After having served for over ten years on its Executive Committee she was appointed chairman in 1962 and then became president in 1964. Her presidential address was entitled 'Travel under Concern', and she talked mainly about the travels of 17th century Friends. After her death Friends likened Elfrida's international travels to some of those undertaken by early Friends. The lecture was repeated later that year in Kendal.

CHAPTER 8

International Travels

NINETEEN FIFTY saw the first of Elfrida's several visits to North America. She was asked if she would let her name go forward as a London Yearly Meeting representative to the Five Years Meeting which was to be held in Richmond, Indiana. She had met and got to know numerous American Friends as a result of her work with the 1652 Committee and had for some time felt she would like to travel among them. Hearing her speak, and realising her deep knowledge of the history of Quakerism, many had invited her to cross the Atlantic and visit them. At first she thought this would be impossible. Her father was ill and couldn't be left for long periods; Percy was also not in the best of health; she herself was only just recovering from a period of back trouble; she was also in the middle of writing her next novel; and what about the dogs? She asked for time to consider this request and to work out whether it might be possible and whether it would be right for her to accept this commitment. Somehow her difficulties were resolved and she became convinced that she should go. The family and the meeting rallied round, and off she went.

She immediately felt at home among programmed[10] Friends in Indiana and her Christocentric approach to Quakerism was greatly valued. Also her ability to talk about the beliefs of 17th century Quakers in a way that showed the connections between the different branches of American Friends, was much appreciated. She always made it plain that she realised that she had something to learn from all branches of Friends and even in

---

10. Quakers who have more structure in their meetings for worship than those in the UK and who also sing hymns. However, they usually have part of their meetings devoted to silent worship like UK Quakers.

the 1980s she said,

> I have not come to an end of the lessons which may be learnt from the richly-flowering branches of Quakerism on these shores, but I thank God for the spiritual fellowship I have enjoyed and the spiritual inspiration I have experienced.

This humility won her many friends and she was invited back on several occasions.

In 1955 she was asked if she would return to give two prestigious lectures. The first was in Richmond again. This time her visit to the Five Years Meeting was not just as a representative but as a visiting lecturer delivering a keynote speech – the Johnson Lecture. Elfrida's title was *'Quaker Witness: Yesterday and Today'*. She reminded her audience of George Fox's vision of an ocean of darkness and death which could be conquered by the ocean of light and love which God could bring about. She spoke of the witness of early Friends in the 17th century and their strong belief that they had a teacher in Jesus Christ and related this to the then current international situation - also speaking of the prophetic utterances of John Wilhelm Rowntree and Rufus Jones. Although she did comment on divisions among Friends, she tactfully used 19th century British examples and not the American divisions. She said 'it is time the old wounds were healed in the only way in which it is possible for them to be healed, in a renewal of our spiritual fellowship.' She ended with her favourite 'dry bones' quotation from Ezekiel.

Afterwards she stayed in the USA and travelled to Pennsylvania to deliver the William Penn Lecture to Young Friends in Philadelphia on 13 November. This annual lecture had been founded (in 1916) 'because Young Friends feel there is a need for their message to be heard and considered' and her brief was to 'challenge thinking and inspire personal search'. Her title was *'Living in the Kingdom'* and again she drew her examples mainly from 17th century Quakers – tracing the story back to John Camm's farmhouse in Cumbria, his conversion to Quakerism at Preston Patrick, his subsequent mission to Oxford, and his conversion of Thomas Loe who in turn convinced William Penn. However, she did not remain in the 17th century. Her message here was for the present. She emphasised both that 'we cannot take up our Quaker heritage at second hand' and also that there is a need for spiritual discipline. 'Our own generation', she said 'is surely due for some hard thinking about discipline in all its aspects.' Many of the examples she quoted were from the arts and from her own early experiences of the necessity for discipline in that field.

On her first visit to the USA, Elfrida had quickly trained herself to write wherever she happened to be – on trains, planes or in airports. She always travelled with several small notebooks. However, this was just an extension of earlier training. Many years ago she had learnt to use every spare minute in her busy life as a wife and mother to write, and said later that 'instead of getting irritated about the countless and inevitable interruptions, I made myself treat them as something life was bringing to me rather than a taking away of time and thought.'

Although she had felt it was right for her to cross the Atlantic, Elfrida had been apprehensive before she went and had wondered what sort of reception she would receive. She need not have worried. She was very impressed and 'warmed by the hospitality she received'. In an interview she gave for the *Christian Science Monitor* when she returned, she said, 'I made up my mind never to refuse to speak about America. Perhaps this was one way to repay American hospitality – especially the simple hospitality that welcomed me right into the family and even into the kitchen.'

As always, Elfrida not only received letters from her young fans, but she also replied to them - often giving some indication of her own feelings and experience. In March 1956 she wrote:

> I congratulate you most warmly on your magazine and long may it flourish! My friends and I used to have a magazine; we wrote it all out by hand, which was rather hard work, but we got a lot of fun out of it. I think we first had the idea after reading 'Little Women', which was one of our favourite story books. Those of you who had read it may be interested to know that when I was in Boston a few months ago, one of the first things I asked was whether I might see the Alcott house in Concord where the author of 'Little Women' lived. It is a museum .... Characters in books go on living you know; the March girls, Jim Hawkins, Alice in Wonderland,

Mowgli and many another are as alive today as they were when the books were written.

She soon received another invitation to cross the Atlantic Ocean – this time to Canada. On 23 June 1957 she delivered the Sunderland P Gardiner Lecture during Canadian Yearly Meeting at Pickering College, Ontario. She impressed the Yearly Meeting, not just with what she had to say, but because she spoke entirely without notes. The report in *The Friend (6.9.57)* was prepared from the notes one of the Friends in her audience had made during her address. Her title was '*Quakerism, a sacramental way of life*' and she began with a story about a young missionary doctor who was engaged in prayer as he walked ahead of his companions through the jungle. A gorilla broke through the undergrowth and his friends, who were too far away to reach him, could only pray. The young doctor continued to walk steadily on his way and the gorilla, after hesitating for a moment, fell in beside him. They walked side by side until they reached a fork in the road when the doctor took one path and the gorilla the other. The doctor's friends were convinced that God had been his companion and had protected him from harm. Elfrida elaborated this theme with illustrations from early Quakers who had felt strongly that God was with them in what they were called to do and remained with them when they suffered in prison. She said that when she was asked about the Quaker attitude to the sacraments, she would reply that Friends' contribution to the Christian Church should not be to denigrate the symbols that mean so much to others. The Quaker testimony should be to the great truth that underlies the sacraments – we should point behind the symbols to the living reality. For example, when we break bread with one another, we experience Holy Communion. We must have faith that God is there and that we can work with him. We must let our lives speak.

In 1958, soon after returning home from Canada, Elfrida was invited to visit Australia and New Zealand. She began her visit in Perth, then touched down in Melbourne before going on to Hobart to open the Quaker College; then back to Melbourne; a short visit to Adelaide; two days in Canberra and finishing up in Sydney. Quite a journey! In Melbourne she

....was interested to learn of the concern for the aborigines felt by Friends in this Meeting and in all the Australian Meetings I visited, and of the work undertaken on their behalf by various members.

While she was staying in Hobart she spoke to pupils at the Friends School, telling them of her family connection with the school – her uncle, Alfred H Brown had been headmaster there for a short time. He had sent home glowing accounts of the State and had aroused her interest in Tasmania. Also in Hobart she 'deeply appreciated the times of worship we shared together and the informal gatherings in homes and with groups.'

After leaving Sydney Elfrida travelled on to spend two weeks in New Zealand. Again she had a hectic schedule, visiting Friends in Christchurch, Oamaru, Dunedin, Wellington and Auckland. But, as in Australia, she found time to talk to the younger generation – not only to pupils at the Friends School in Wanganui but also those at Otago High School and Queen's High School in Dunedin. She told them she 'spent long hours each day writing and had no time for morning or afternoon teas'. In an article she wrote for *The Friend* she expressed concern at the low level of staffing at Friends School and said 'Young Friends who are interested in Quaker experiments in education, and in the prospects of life overseas, would do well to inquire as to the existing vacancies, whether on the teaching or household staff.'

Elfrida did not only speak to Quakers and school children on her travels, she also promoted her books. Signings and press interviews were arranged in most of the major towns and cities she visited. The *Canberra Times* on 11.11.58 reported

> The values the world of children's books fostered could help to maintain standards and combat the evil influences of the real world. As a child she (Elfrida) had been taken to the home of Beatrix Potter in the English Lake District, and had fancied she saw there Peter Rabbit and his friends. As an adult, she had visited Louisa May Alcott's house at Concord, USA, and had sensed the presence of the 'little women' who had been that author's inspiration.'

And on 29.11.58 the *Dunedin Star* noted that Elfrida was 'a woman who brought back to children's books a religious quality after this had almost completely disappeared in the 1920s following overemphasis in the Victorian era.'

She hoped to write books for children about Australia and New Zealand, realising that many of the books children used there had UK backgrounds, scenery and themes. She collected much material with a view to doing this – not only relating to Quaker stories. She noted that in 1768 Captain Cook's ship, the Endeavour, carried the first Friend ever to visit New Zealand – Sydney Parkinson, a botanical draughtsman who died on the homeward journey but not until after he had produced more than 1,300 sketches and meticulously executed paintings of botanical specimens gathered by the expedition botanists. She collected quantities of material on the voyage of the May family to South Australia in 1839. She was also able to do some research there for a book she was hoping to write on James Backhouse, a Quaker who had travelled to Australia in 1831 to investigate conditions among convicts and aborigines. She often referred to James Backhouse in the many lectures she gave, but no more substantial publication was produced. Alas none of these potentially fascinating books ever materialised

Elfrida was a committed member of Yealand Women's Institute and also of the WI's sister body, Associated Country Women of the World. In her term of office as president of the Yealand WI, she had enjoyed helping to organise a local WI festival exhibition and contributed an old Quaker wedding dress. In New Zealand, in addition to her literary and Quaker engagements, she also spoke at a meeting of the Associated Country Women of the World in Christchurch. When she was in Australia she spoke to a similar meeting in Hobart.

In 1965 Elfrida was back in the USA and stayed for a term at Pendle Hill, a Quaker study centre near Philadelphia. During that time she gave a series of ten talks there and also a lecture in Philadelphia entitled 'The Faith to Live By'. In addition, she travelled to Indiana to speak at Richmond again.

Her next visit to the USA was made in September/October 1976. This time she took with her a set of slides of the 1652 country and gave illustrated talks to a number of Quaker Schools, to Meetings and to retirement homes. A Friend reporting on a Pendle Hill conference Elfrida spoke at wrote:

Elfrida spoke on her belief that the only Friend is a convinced Friend, whether one comes to Q by birth or choice. She told of how she came to her own convincement through the experience of art. Hard work was necessary, she stressed; one needed dedication and self-sacrifice to achieve art, and humility and courage. Elfrida said she learned after years of seeking that she was not learning just a theory of art but about life itself. She had discovered the faith of her forefathers - that consciousness of the Inner Light - by her own route. Its expression is the whole of life, and the forging of the links of faith is a life-long process. Elfrida believes that there are many doors to finding faith, and that we must hold seekers in our love as they look for their own doors.

She was back again in 1977 but this time to visit Minneapolis. It was on this visit that she made contact with the Kerlan Collection in the library there and this led to continuing correspondence and eventually to Elfrida sending them some of her manuscripts. Afterwards she called in at Wichita and Kansas and then flew on to Canada – to Toronto and Kingston. She was delighted to meet with two of her former Yealand Manor pupils in Canada – Tim Benson and Janet (Croker) West.

The next visit was in 1982 and this time she stayed with Friends belonging to the most evangelical wing of Quakerism. Although some Friends in Britain Yearly Meeting have difficulty in relating to this branch of Quakerism, Elfrida did not share their doubts. Perhaps this was because she constantly referred back to 17th century Friends – who were considerably more evangelical and Christocentric than Britain Yearly Meeting Friends today.

On that visit she stayed and talked at George Fox College, Oregon, at Friends University in Wichita, Kansas and at William Penn College, Oskaloose in Iowa.

It was also at this time that she was asked to write short biographies of early Quakers for the American publication *Quaker Life*. Starting in April 1983 these appeared every month until December 1985.

The Pendle Hill Pamphlet No. 248 entitled *The Candle of the Lord* and printed in 1983 was her last major publication. In this she continued to draw on the lives of 17th century Quakers, but in addition she wrote about her own personal experience. She recognised the influence that Rufus Jones had had on her thinking and was grateful to a Friend at Pendle Hill who had told her about his favourite quotation. She wrote:

> I owe many happy memories to Pendle Hill: memories of new friendships and shared experiences, of the inspiration of worship and of beauty, of music on the lips and echoing in the heart, of the sublime refreshment of nonsense... I deeply revered Rufus Jones and he is still a constant source of inspiration to me, but never more than in this favourite text: 'The spirit of man is the candle of the Lord.'

Her last transatlantic visit was made in 1984. By this time Elfrida was far from well, but she had been awarded an Honorary Degree from Earlham College and she was determined to receive this in person. She arrived three days before the ceremony, but instead of resting spoke at Earlham School of Religion and to various gatherings of Indiana Friends, many of whom had visited the 1652 country and had heard her speak at Swarthmoor Hall. At the ceremony on 3 June she was presented for the degree by Hugh Barbour who said, among other things, 'her friends at Earlham College delight to complete the circle of her life by a scholar's degree' – referring, perhaps to the fact that she never completed her degree at Manchester University all those years ago. She was awarded the Honorary Degree of Doctor of Humane Letters by the President of the College (President DeWitt C Baldwin) who said

> Elfrida Vipont Foulds, writer whose words have delighted and instructed generations of readers, interpreter of Quakerism to countless seekers, religious teacher through your words and your example, you have given the greatest gift anyone can offer the human community, the personal witness of a life-long search for and commitment to the truth. In and through you Earlham College pays honour to the Quaker foundations on which it rests.

It was a splendid end to her international travels.

Epilogue

ELFRIDA'S LAST years were saddened by a series of strokes. She died in March 1992, leaving her four daughters, thirteen grandchildren and nine great-grandchildren. In her Quaker Testimony it is noted that

> It would be comparatively easy to catalogue all that Elfrida did. It is what she was that so endeared her to us. But what she was needs to be seen in the context of her activities, which were wide ranging in scope and demanding in nature.

She is buried in Yealand Quaker burial ground, with Percy and her Parents. On a clear day there is a splendid view of Ingleborough and the Pennine hills from there. Those who visit may remember the psalm she often quoted:

> I will lift up mine eyes to the hills,
> from whence cometh my help.
> My help cometh from the Lord,
> who made heaven and earth
> *(Psalm 121)*

Elfrida at Earlham College, receiving her Honorary Degree

This picture and the cover photograph are reproduced by courtesy of the University Librarian & Director, the John Rylands Library, the University of Manchester

Appendix

ELFRIDA'S PUBLISHED WORKS
not including contributions made to joint publications (except for the first item) or published lectures

1930	Mount Street (Manchester) 1830-1930 (two chapters)
1931	Good Adventure: The Quest of Music in England
1934	Colin writes to Friends House
1938	Lift up your lamps
1939	Blow the Man Down (*Charles Vipont*)
1948	The Lark in the Morn
1950	The Lark on the Wing (**Carnegie Medal**)
1950	Sparks among the Stubble
1950	A Lily among Thorns: some passages in the life of Margaret Fell
1952	The Birthplace of Quakerism: a handbook for the 1652 country
1954	Let your Lives Speak (Pendle Hill pamphlet 71)
1954	The Story of Quakerism
1955	The Heir of Craigs (*Charles Vipont*)
1955	The Family at Dowbiggins
1955	Arnold Rowntree: a Life
1957	The High Way (anthology)
1957	The Spring of the Year
1957	The Secret of Orra
1958	More about Dowbiggins (Reprinted 1968 as A Win for Henry Conyers)
1958	Bless This Day - a book of prayer for children (anthology)
1959	Ackworth School (Reprinted 1991 edition with additional chapters)
1959	Henry Purcell and his Times
1960	Changes at Dowbiggins (Reprinted 1969 as Boggarts & Dreams)
1960	The Story of Christianity in Britain

1960 Flowering Spring
1961 What about Religion?
1962 The Bridge (anthology)
1962 Search for a Song
1963 Some Christian Festivals
1965 The Offcomers
1965 Quakerism - A Faith to Live By
1965 Larry Lopkins
1965 Rescue for Mittens
1965 Stevie
1966 Weaver of Dreams (*Charlotte Brontë*)
1966 Ghosts High Noon (Reprinted 1969 as Terror by Night)
1967 The Secret Passage
1967 The China Dog
1967 A Child of the Chapel Royal
1969 Michael and the Dogs
1969 The Pavilion
1969 Children of the Mayflower
1969 The Elephant and the Bad Baby
1970 Towards a High Attic (*George Eliot*)
1974 Bed in Hell
1975 George Fox and the Valiant Sixty
1977 A Little Bit of Ivory (*Jane Austen*)
1979 Swarthmoor Hall
1983 The Candle of the Lord (Pendle Hill pamphlet 248)